CW00433530

C(

Chapter 1: The Fallen girl

My name is Eileen Miller in 1948, at the age of sixteen I was sent to a Magdalene laundry in Belfast, and my life was changed forever. `

I decided at the age of eighty-six, I wanted to view places I worked at and lived throughout my life, looking back on the journey I went through during my life. I started at Helen's hospital, in Dublin, where I studied as a shy student nurse at the age of nineteen, to becoming a matron of a general medical ward managing a team of thirty staff.

I missed being with patients in their darkest times, at the point of being told of their cancer diagnosis, to hold their hands during their final moments, a privilege and an honor.

After visiting the hospital, I travelled to St Bernadett's laundry, the institution I was sent to at the age of sixteen for having a child out of wedlock. The laundry was now burnt down, and derelict, and after taking a deep breath it took me all my strength to enter, to relieve the horror I experienced.

The building was in the middle of a derelict field, three stories high, with smashed windows and I could observe the rotten thornbush on the side of the building. I nervously walked along the cobbled path, to the black wooden doors, and as I opened the door, I observed the dark, gloomy, and creepy corridor. At the end of the corridor was a large Victorian mirror smashed on the floor. I remember looking into the mirror in between working in the workhouse, observing my tired and worn-out expression. I looked through the great hall and could see that it was now rubble.

I could still remember the long row of tables the taste of the stale and lumpy porridge, and the sound of the nun's shouting for us to 'hurry up' and the prayers we completed in unison every morning, afternoon, and night. I then walked up the rotten golden staircase, which was now covered in broken glass leading to the dormitories. As I looked into the dormitory room, I could see that the beds were stacked up in a pile. I stood by the window, observing the beautiful scenic mountains and beautiful fields. Looking out of the window reminded me of the prison I was in, and I felt like a teenager again, lost scared and frightened. Some scars never heal, and I could still feel the trauma I held inside me, a harrowing experience of being punished, bullied, and vilified, feelings that would go onto shape my entire life.

After visiting the laundry, I took the train to my childhood home, in Barrett Lane in Donegal, a place I lived in before my innocence was taken away. The house had now been burnt down and all that remained was rubble.

I lived in the stone cottage with my parents, my six brothers and five sisters. My Father John delivered newspapers, and my mother Janet was an assistant library in the local town. We were extremely poor, and I shared one bed with my sisters. At dinner we would eat scraps of bread and cold soup, and in the morning before we went to school, we would take it in turns to walk to the water fountain and collect water in containers.

Despite the poverty we lived in, we were happy together in our own world, playing games together, singing songs on the way to school, and our bond and love for each other pulled us through the darkest times.

Jack was my eldest brother and had a place in Belfast university to study medicine, Tom was the second oldest brother had had decided to move to Australia to work for a finance company, finally obtaining a ticket out of poverty. James was my twin brother, but we were polar opposites, whilst I was shy and reserved James was outgoing, popular, and the class clown, we were incredibly close, and always looked out for each other.

Malachy and Dominic were my youngest brothers aged six and seven, and they were constantly getting up to mischief, chasing after animals, putting spiders in our bed, and shouting at the teachers at school. Lewis was the baby of the family at six months of age.

Mena was my closest sister, and like James, she had a childish nature, and would often ride on our horse to school or let off firecrackers.

Edith was my older sister, and was kind and caring, and was the cook of the family, and could make a dinner for the family with the smallest of ingredients. Minnie was the eldest sister and a real mother to us all, working in a toy factory, she was the breadwinner, she filled the house with toys and gifts for us all, when we had so little.

Cath was my younger sister, and had a disruptive personality, and would often start fights, pulling our hair and punching my other sisters, and had a very volatile personality.

Helena was the singer of the family and would always sing to us, her favorite singer was Elvis and she enjoyed memorizing his songs, she would sing at the dinner table on the way to school, or at night.

I always felt we were happy despite our poverty, we had each other, and took pleasure from just being close together.

On 30th August, at the age of fifteen, I stood at the gate of our house with my siblings as we waved goodbye to Tom. Tom was dressed in his green overcoat and carried a small satchel and was ready to say goodbye to his home in Ireland and make his way to the airport to Australia. We were crying, as we watched him ride his bike into the glare of the sun. Tom had taught me to ride a bike, and helped me learn to read, and now he was gone, we were a close-knit family, and we knew the loss of Tom would leave a major hole.

I walked upstairs to get changed into my sweatshirt and trousers, there were hole in my clothes and the soles of my shoes were ripped. I could hear Helena singing, 'you aint nothing but a houndog,' even in the darkest of times she used music to make light of the situation.

I walked down the cobbled road with Mena and Mal, and Dom, as we made our way to the county fair.

"Why are we taking these two to the fair? Last year they burst the bouncy castle and set off the sprinklers."

"They love it, and it will keep them out of trouble," I urged.

"Tell the truth you are going to see your Derek, you are totally obsessed with him," Mena laughed.

"I have to make the most of my time with Derek, he is moving to London in a month, who knows I may not see him again," I sighed.

I had been courting Derek for a year, he was seventeen years old, a laborer and we were inseparable for the entire year we were together, we would go for long walks together on Sunday mornings, we would travel to Belfast, and spend an afternoon in the arcades on Saturday's.

The fare was magnificent, with a bright colorful Ferris wheel, bumper cars, a fun house, and the waltzes. It felt wonderful being on the Ferris wheel with Derek, I was so young and carefree unaware that my life was about to change dramatically.

"Will you write to me when you go to England? Life will be so miserable without you!"

"Of course, I will write to you, I will be home every two months, there is no one like you," He smiled.

As Mena took my brothers on the assortment of rides we went on the bumper cars together,

"I am so sorry to tell you, but it is true," she

muttered, I felt my hands shaking, and my heart

was pounding against my chest, it would be

observed as a terrible sin, and I knew my parents

would fly into rage.

I felt confused, and a part of me wanted to run

away, but I knew my options were limited.

"Please Dr Carver don't tell my parents that I'm

pregnant! They will kill me and make my life hell!"

I pleaded.

"Ok," Dr Carver muttered, I should not have

trusted her, I was naïve, sixteen, and my life had

been turned upside down.

The summer had ended, and a month later I was ready to start my final year of school. I wore baggy clothes and was worried incase anyone would spot my growing bump, I felt like a ticking time bomb, and the net was closing in on me. I stood in the mirror in my uniform with the towering cardigan covering my body.

I walked along to school with James, and he knelt, and I jumped onto his shoulders, it was one of our traditions for him to carry me on the first day. I enjoyed these moments knowing that my life was about to change forever, then as we continued down the cobbled road, we observed the most beautiful black horse in the field.

I watched in horror as James jumped onto the horse.

"C'mon join me!" He cheered.

"You must be joking I can't!"

It was then that James carried me and put me onto the horse before climbing onto the front. To my horror, the horse jolted forward, and I held onto James. I felt so free in that moment, the crisp hot sun on my face, the wind brushing past my skin, and I laughed all the way to school, as we jumped over haystacks and into shallow pools of water. It was the last time I had laughed whole heatedly.

I arrived at school at 9am, I went to a co ed school 'St Mary's' it was a strict catholic school, we had to line up at 9am for a uniform inspection. Our class teacher a nun called Sister Eleanor was very strict, I remember her wearing a dark cloak, her hair was long, greasy, and knotted, her face was wrinkled, and she had a long-pointed nose resembling a witch.

I observed Bertie my best friend, she was rebellious, carefree, and always pulling pranks on the teachers, I admired her resilience, her bravery and her courage. Bertie was five foot two, with red curly hair, and would wear makeup although it was prohibited.

We sat in English in the cold, dark, gloomy bathroom, the curtains were drawn, and the chairs were small and uncomfortable, and the desks nearly crushed us as we leaned forward.

Sister Eleoner set us work to read a 'Charles Dickens book' in silence, it was torture, it was an exercise of cruelty, if we dared breathe or make a noise she would make life hell for us, she was able to spot misbehavior with her back turned. Bertie could always be relied on to cause trouble she handed me a screwed-up note, I opened it and began to laugh immediately, she had drawn a cartoon image of Sister Eleoner and the words, 'stupid cow' written on top.

I watched as a furious Sister Eleanor stormed towards me, and grabbed the note and immediately clasped her eyes on Bertie.

"Eileen and Bertie see me after class!" She yelled.

I knew this spelled trouble, and I watched after class, in terror, as she made Bertie kneel on the floor, she knelt stony face, almost immune to caning after having so many beatings, I was spared on this one occasion, but the verbal berate was just as damaging.

"Look at you Eileen, standing there, pretty as a picture, looking like butter wouldn't melt, but we all know about you, your secret courting with Derek, the local tramp farmer, you're heading to the laundry along with Bertie," She scowled.

"Fucking hell," Bertie whispered.

"What did you say?" Sister Eleoner ordered.

"I said God's sake," She smiled, before sticking her middle finger up at Sister Eleoner behind her back.

As I walked out of the school, with Bertie we passed by the laundry, the prison to hundreds of young women. Beyond the golden spiked bars, I observed the tall rundown building, with vines crawling around the edges, and metal bars on the window given a prison feel.

From the gates we observed the women in the laundry room, dressed in their brown dirty rags, and a white cotton cloth over their heads. We watched as the women were standing over the large basins, cleaning the dirty laundry as the steam evaporated around the room. I could see the frail expression on the women, their pale faces, their clothes resembled death shrouds. A shudder ran through me, I knew there was the possibility I could be in the asylum, and suffer the same fate, and I was petrified, no one knew my secret not even Derek.

I walked home and watched in horror as I observed Dr Carver leaving my driveway, I felt my heart sink.

I observed my father outside digging deep into the mud.

"Da how are you?" I asked.

Dad ignored me, as he carried on digging, then as I crept into the house matters were about to worsen.

My mother was sitting at the table with a rowel in her hand sobbing, her face was worn, and she was shivering.

"I can't believe you have done this to us you have destroyed your father Eileen, you were so sensible, you were meant to go on to become a nurse, this is going to destroy your life."

"No, I can still have a life it is not over yet, I have so much to give."

"We can't tell your siblings, we'll have to get you wearing ill-fitting clothes, you'll have the baby in secret,"

"You won't throw me out! You won't send me to the laundry!" I pleaded.

"I suggest you keep away from your father, he is furious with you, you will have this baby in secret, we can't afford anyone in the town to find out, it will be the city shame, you are forbidden to tell anyone."

I ran upstairs, in anger, and collapsed onto the bed in tears, and I knew the next few months were going to be very difficult, but the road ahead was going to be much worse.

I spent most of my days after, wearing heavy jumpers' and baggy trousers, there were many days when I was too sick to go to school, and my brother and sisters were more concerned than suspicious about my strange behavior.

I had tried desperately to cover my pregnancy, and then seven months into my pregnancy disaster struck. I was in excruciating pain in my math class and ran with all my might into the girl's bathroom, and then it happened, my waters broke. I was terrified, and I began to scream, I screamed so loud, and the worst person in the entire world was alerted to my shouts, Sister Eleoner.

I looked on as Sister Eleanor's face she looked on in terror.

"Oh my God, what in the lord's name?"

I watched as she ran out maliciously, as I screamed out in pain, I was in labor, I was shocked to see her compassion as she returned with towels and hot water. After half an hour and after unbearable pain and suffering, my 7-pound baby boy, I named John was born. I can still remember how tiny he looked wrapped in a white towel, as I held him, I could see a vulnerable helpless child looking up at me, and I instantly felt the love from this wonderful child, after months of heartache and I began to cry profusely.

The ambulance team arrived, and they helped me onto the stretcher as a paramedic took the baby away. As I exited the bathroom and they wheeled me down the corridor, the girls in the school lined up at the side of the corridor, and I could feel their beady eyes looking at me, the laughs, the look of shock, the whispers, I felt like a test subject.

Just before I was wheeled into the ambulance, Bertie appeared, "I'm her sister, I'm coming with her!" she pleaded.

As the ambulance carried me away to the hospital, I continued to cry through the glass I could see that it was raining heavily, my heart was pounding, I was terrified for what was to come, I had a terrible feeling inside of impending doom.

"Why didn't you tell me you silly bitch! I could have helped you!" Bertie yelled.

I could not speak, I was bereft with anticipatory grief, wondering what my fate was.

I arrived at the hospital and was put in a cold clinical room with white walls and a glass wall. Standing behind the glass was my mother, crying, looking at me with disgust whilst my father had his back turned, talking to a doctor.

"Where Is my Baby?" I asked the nurse, she looked at me like an alien, like I did not matter.

It was clear that the baby was taken away, and that no one would let me see him, I felt completely hopeless.

An hour after my hospital assessment a ward orderly helped me into a wheelchair, I wore a blue nightgown and white slippers. As we exited the room, my parents continued to turn their backs, I called out their names, but they ignored me. The orderly took me outside and I observed a black van and two guards dressed in black.

Suddenly my sisters Minnie and Mena appeared, they were crying and shaking as they stood by the black cab. I struggled as I stood from the wheelchair, and I embraced them both together.

"C'mon Miss get in the car," yelled the guard.

"Where am I going?" I yelled.

The two guards grabbed me forcefully into the car, I felt like a criminal as I began to scream. I looked out of the window and could see the disgruntled faces of my parents, and the devastation etched on my sisters' faces.

I watched them disappear as we drove out of the car park, and they faded in the sun.

I knew in my heart that I was being taken to the Magdalene laundry, I had expected it for months and my life was being stripped away from me.

As I closed my eyes in the back of the cab, I thought about my final summer at home, watching Mal and Dom setting fire to the barn, and Mena letting the chicken's loose, and my Aunty Minnie returned from Belfast with a bag of toys. It was a magical time, a time of innocence, a time that would soon become a memory.

Chapter 2: Entering Hell

The rain poured heavily, as the guards dragged me out of the car, and I gained my first look at the laundry. The building was tall and creepy with vines growing from the side, the windows were rotten with bars and the oak trees at the front gave a creepy feel. It looked like prison, a place where people were punished.

Standing at the door was Sister Abbie a wicked looking nun with long black hair, wearing a long black clock, "here comes trouble," she muttered. Standing next to her was Sister Elizabeth a young nun with blonde hair aged 26, I was to find that she was a servant to Abbie and would follow her every word.

As I stood on the doorstep, I was drenched, wet, cold and freezing, I felt like an insect as Elizabeth looked through me with her cold green eyes.

"Come with me, walk straight, and with your back straight, "She ordered, as I walked down the pitch-black corridor, as they guided me up the creaking rotten stairs.

We reached the second floor, a row of dormitories containing over a hundred fallen girls.

"Right Eileen this will be your room, you'll find your night dress and work clothes hanging at the end of the bed, breakfast is at 6am and work duties start at 7am. "

"Work duties?" I asked.

"Anyway, no more questions you better get to bed." Elizabeth pestered.

I stepped into the cold, lonely room, the girls in the room were sleeping on the hard wooden bed, with just a single sheet covering them. I walked over to the window and looked outside, the full moon lit up the sky, and the stars sparkled. It looked magical and I had just entered hell, in that moment I took solace, the moon and stars were my only comfort.

I awoke the next morning, after 5am, and I met Anita, a 30 year old woman, who had been in the laundry for over fourteen years, she was the strongest person I knew, and the mother to all the other girls, and a person who I could confide in when I felt low.

Rita was sixteen, and a rebel, and was sent to the laundry after setting fire to her local church, Rita was not very talkative and held a lot of hatred towards the nun's, constantly testing the waters by talking back to them, and completing pranks.

Lucy was seventeen and sent to the asylum by her teacher, a nun, who had a vendetta against her, jealous of her good looks, her tall height, and her sporting ability, she was one of the strongest girl's I had met, it was an injustice that she was sent to the laundry.

Bernadette was twenty-four and was given an allowance not to partake in work duties due to her reclusive behavior. I now believe Bernadette was autistic, and her behavioral outbursts were mistaken for intentional bad behavior.

Jenny was seventeen, and rarely spoke, she was sent to the asylum after giving birth to twins, and was in such a deep depression she would often be found at night, laying in her bed crying, living in deep trauma from the loss of her children.

I put on my grey uniform and black plimsole shoes, I felt like a slave, it was five sizes too big for me, and I had become the person I dreaded my whole life.

"Stay positive, don't talk during chores, and say yes to everything, they prey on vulnerability," Anita warned.

"How have you survived here for fourteen years?"

"I've had no choice, my family have disowned me there's no hope of my family ever getting me out, but you have to live in hope."

"In hope? Why lie to her? This place is a prison! You will never get out of here, the nun's here have tight surveillance around here, and if you attempt to leave, well it's a fate you won't recover from!" Rita scowled.

I walked over to the long vanity mirror in the corner of the room, it was the only vanity product we had, apart from a rusty piece of soap we had to share between us. I looked on and had to hold my tears in and bit my lip, I closed my eyes and imagined my siblings sitting at the kitchen table eating an English breakfast.

I look in the mirror now and see an 86-year-old survivor, with wrinkles, grey worn hair and mental scars which have never disappeared.

My living room is now filled with boxes, full of memories, including books, clothes and gadgets, which help to alleviate my mood when I felt low, it is so hard to let go of memories. My most prized and cherished possession was the nurse outfit, it marked my escape, my ability to break free from poverty and enter a life where I could establish financial freedom.

Chapter 3: Laundry life

We entered the great hall which had over twenty rows of tables, it felt like I was at school, although in the laundry we were under strict supervision and were encouraged to be silent. I sat next to Anita, and watched as the nun's came to each girl and poured the sticky lumpy porridge into the bowl, the porridge tasted like paste and made me feel sick. I watched as the nun's sat at a table in the corner of the room, with their hot porridge and cornflakes and steaming hot cups of tea, it felt like an act of cruelty, they wanted us to suffer.

After breakfast, we were then ordered into the laundry rooms to complete our work duties. I was overwhelmed, as soon as I walked into the room there were over forty basins one for each girl, and next to the bowls were piles of dirty linen for us to clean. This method of work was seen as purging our sins, and a way for us to be forgiven, in the same way as Mary Magdalene.

We each had a gritty piece of soap, and the water in the bowl was so hot our hands were often left red and sore after a day's work. I attempted to speak to Louise, the girl next to me, a 15-year-old girl, who had given birth to a child out of wedlock over a year ago. I was trying to keep my sanity, speaking to someone else to try and get me through the twelve-hour shift, but sister Elizabeth caught us talking.

"There is no room for talking in the laundry from midday, you will both be required to meet me at

the corridor and scrub the floors as punishment,"
She yelled.

Then at twelve, we shared a bucket of water and held a ripped flannel, and we began to scrub on our hands and knees, and I felt my knees rip, and start to bleed. We were ordered to clean the filthy stairs and we could feel the shadow of a nun hanging over us, making sure we completed the job to perfection. We only had one plastic cup filled with water which would last us the entire day.

After we completed the shift, we were called into Sister Elizabeth's office, and we were ordered to kneel at the foot of her desk, and we watched in horror as Sister Elizabeth walked towards the cabinet to collect her steel came. It was then that she began to whip us repeatedly, we must have been hit over twenty times, it was a depraved act, committed out of cruelty, I held my breath to get through it. I felt like I was in prison, I felt like the nun's were trying to grind me down and push me to breaking point.

As I walked out of the room, I observed Rita being taken away by the guards, pulled away under her arms, to solitary confinement. Rita had refused to take part in chores, and she was being sent to the basement. The worst place in the asylum, situated on the ground floor, with steel bars, swarming with rats, we were all warned about the place, and the impeccable behavior required to avoid it.

It took all my strength to hold my head up in the dormitory, to lie about where I had been. Little things in the dormitory kept my heart up, such as Lucy's Elvis book, hidden deep beneath the cracks of the floorboards. It was a wonderful way to escape the asylum and get lost in the book filled with Hollywood lights and Elvis's extravagant lifestyle.

I looked after Bernadette, each night, she was so weak, I would help her to wash at the sink and to clean her hair. I felt like I was Bernadette's carer, the nuns were not aware of her growing needs, she was vulnerable and scared, I tried so hard to look after her, but tried to conceal the caring relationship from the nuns who would take it out on me.

Days past, and I spent so much of my time thinking of my family especially at night. I missed the morning breakfast, playing in the field and the songs we would sing together. I missed normal routine, life, laughing with my siblings, and being a carefree teenager.

Then, one hot August afternoon, we were outside in the courtyard, I heard a familiar voice calling my name, as I looked to the gate, I observed Mena, standing in a red coat, with a little box, and tears falling down her cheeks.

I ran over to her, quickly, and held onto her hands.

"I miss you so much, but if they see you talking to me, I'll get into serious trouble."

"Mother will forgive you soon, I am working on her, one day very soon, I promise to get you out of here, but I have this little gift in a box for you, some of your favorite photos, take them but be sure to hide them," she warned.

I quickly took the box of black and white photos and put them in my pocket, hoping that the nuns would never find them.

I went up to the dormitory and sat under the window and the light of the moonlight lit up the photobook. I marveled at the pictures, including the photo of us all sitting in the hay with my parents, laughing and singing. Then there was a photo of me burying Mal and Dom in the sand, whilst another photo showed us standing at the front of our church, at Christmas, with Mena throwing the fake baby Jesus into the air. All of the photos brought back happy memories to me and made me long even more to be at home. I found a small hole in the floorboards, and I was able to hide the box in secret. It was my secret and I felt powerful keeping it, like I had a certain power over the nun's.

As I lay in the cold, lumpy and creaky bed, I thought about my son, in my mind I named him John. I often wondered if I would ever meet him, if he would still be a child, or if I would meet him in later adulthood. I had to hope I would get my life back and escape the hell.

Chapter 4: Christmas

Christmas was always going to be difficult in the laundry being away from my family, and pondering about the future, feeling lonelier than ever. On 1st December at night, I could hear shuffling in the room, and a dark shadow standing in the corner with a satchel. It was Rita, I could see that she was enraged that she could see me.

"Go back to sleep, this is no concern of yours!" She scowled.

"Where are you going?"

"I'm breaking out of this prison," she scathed.

In a moment of impulsivity, I jumped up from the bed, and put on my overcoat, and work shoes, and tiptoed towards a disgruntled Rita.

"Eileen, I will take the lead, you follow me, but you must not make a sound, if you do, we will both be in great danger," she whispered.

I could feel my heart racing, as we slowly exited the dormitory, we tiptoed down the stairs, both filled with fear, knowing we were both at risk.

Then as we reached the bottom of the stairs, I observed Rita holding the master key to the door, and she charged forward, and I followed suit as she effortlessly unlocked the door, and we made our way to the master gate and unlocked it, reaching a cobbled path. I took off my shoes and ran with all my might, the wind brushed passed my hair and my heart began to race rapidly, there was such an excitement wrapped up in fear in that one moment. I watched as Rita ran, miles ahead, and we reached the forest area.

"Rita!" I muttered, but she never turned around, in the distance I could hear the sirens from the laundry, the sirens which signaled that a girl had escaped the laundry. I knew the guards were coming for me, and I put my shoes on, trudging through the rough leaves and pieces of wood. I found a hidden cave dugout at the top of a steep hill, and I hid inside, that is when I could see Rita hiding behind a tree, out of breath, and gasping for air, I could see her scathing, her hands gripping the mud and throwing it in frustration.

Then I could hear the loud thuds from the guards in their boots, calling out our names, demanding for us to show ourselves. Their voices became distant and then their voices grew close, and I observed the lights from their flashlights hitting the tree, and that is when a guard spotted Rita. The guard ran towards Rita and wrestled her to the ground.

"Get off me you bastard!" She yelled. I watched as she reached her hand forward, and she reached for a rock and hit the guard across the head, knocking him to the ground, and she ran as fast as she could into the distance, she escaped she was finally free.

Then, I felt something crawl over my leg, a rat and I let out a loud gasp before covering my mouth.

"Make it known where you are right now!" yelled the guard.

My heart raced further, I wanted to have the confidence to run, but I was not as quick thinking as Rita, and I watched as a guard knelt in front of me.

"I've got her!" He yelled.

Suddenly I felt a guard at the other end of the cave grabbing my legs, pulling my legs, as I screamed loudly.

As I stood up, both guards held onto my arms.

"Don't tell Sister Elizabeth I beg of you, she will kill me, please spare me!" I begged.

"You chose to leave now you face the consequences," He yelled at me, as the blood trickled down my legs, I was covered in mud, I felt so hopeless.

The guards led me towards the car, and I was in tears, shaking uncontrollably, I wondered if it was possible to die from fear. As I looked outside, I observed the most significant owl, staring at me with the bright orange eyes and looking at me wickedly.

For the first time in months, I began to pray, praying for hope and security, praying for a miracle.

The guards dragged me under my arms towards the laundry.

"Please go easy on me, I'm in pain, my legs are sore, please!" I pleaded.

It was no use, the guards would not listen to me, and my dignity was spared, I'm sure I told them I was thirsty and starving also.

They guided me through the cold, damp, and creepy corridor, and I knew straight away that they were sending me to the basement. As they guided me down the deep stairs, they thew me against the wall, giving me just a small plastic cup of water. The basement was just as I thought it would be, freezing cold, the floor was hard, lumpy, and dusty, in the corner was a rat scurrying around. I had finally lost the glimmer of hope I once held on to. I spent the entire night looking through the broken glass of the window, hoping if there is a God that he would be watching me.

The next morning, I woke up with my back aching and my head filled with pain, the guards swooped in and gave me my cold lumpy porridge, and finally took pity on me, giving me bandages and a warm bowl of water to clean my wounds.

At the time I felt like I was in a kennel, an animal would not be subjected to such abuse. I consumed the porridge, and water, which gave me the burst of energy I needed. The only thing I was grateful was, was being given an exemption for cleaning duties in the workroom.

I felt so bored, as I counted the tiles in the room, desperate to stay awake, and then Sister Elizabeth rushed in, her green evil eyes were glowing into mine as I watched her hold her Cane in her hand.

"Sister Elizabeth, I'm sorry, I'm in pain, please spare me from punishment."

"On your knees, kneel please," she ordered. It was then she subjected me to the most horrendous abuse, whipping me with the Cain across my arms twenty times.

I watched as Sister Elizabeth took off her plimsole and went to hot me.

"Please sister, don't I beg of you."

I watched as she gave me an icy cold stare,

sparing me this one time.

"I promise you Eileen, you pull this trick again,

and 'll finish you, that's a promise!" She scowled.

I did not tell the other girl's about escaping the asylum, it was too traumatic to recall, and I felt empowered to keep secrets, we were unable to have secrets in the asylum, so I felt a sense of power.

Christmas arrived and it was just how I imagined it, dark gloomy and lonely. On Christmas morning we all received an orange on our bad, I was surprised we were given any gifts at all, I think we were all most grateful that we had a day free from laundry duties.

In the morning we had to prepare for the Christmas mass, the nun's had left a red dress and white plimsoles at the end of the bed. The outfit was a charade, the only item we could wear once a year, which was not our slave costume.

At 9am, we lined up outside the laundry, and we walked in unison, in silence, along the cobbled footpath to St Michaels Church. For once we felt human, we were presented well, but our slavery was covered up, the scars on our back, we were mere actors.

We arrived at the church, and were seated at the front, as I turned my head around, I could see my family sitting at the back. My Mother had tears in her eyes and refused to look at me, Mena was in tears, and my father looked on emotionlessly as always. My other sisters gently smiled, whilst Mal and Dom were misbehaving with their toy soldiers. I was happy to see them, It had now been a year they were all growing up, I was growing up in a ball of trauma, and underneath I was a frightened sixteen-year-old desperate for help.

The mass was long, and I refused to listen, I was looking blankly ahead, I was numb to religion after the treatment I endured, I sang an Elvis song to myself to try and get through.

As we walked down the aisle, I walked with a vulnerable Bernadette, I observed her looking at her mother who was wearing a black fluffy hat,

"Mother It's me Bernadette, Mother take me home," Bernadette pleaded.

I watched as Bernadette's mother stood stiff as a board, embarrassed by Bernadette behavior. Sister Elizabeth charged forward to grab her by the hands.

"Let go of your mother, let go of her now, you are in God's house, let her go," She muttered in a stern manner, linking her arms with Bernadette. There was no break from Bernadette steely, aggressive behavior, Christmas certainly was no exemption. As we left the chapel, I tried to get the attention of my parents desperate to get a sympathetic look, but it never come.

We arrived back at the laundry at 3pm, the cooks had prepared over one hundred plates of cold, stale mash, and undercooked chicken. At home we were so poor we would have dreamed of a nourishing roast dinner, and here I was, with the worst meal I had ever tasted.

Sitting on the top table in the corner of the room were the nun's eating their luxurious roast dinners, steam coming from the gravy, we even watched as they were given chocolate pudding for dessert, just when I thought they couldn't stoop any lower they did.

That afternoon we were allowed an hour in the courtyard, I wrapped my coat around me, and sat on the bench overlooking the beautiful dandelions. In the distance I could hear the children singing Christmas carol's including 'hark the herald angels sing,' and 'oh holy night,'

Then I heard the gentle whispers of Mena and James in the background, they were both dressed in their red winter coats with objects in their hands.

"Merry Christmas Sister! Mena smiled, placing a small piece of chocolate cake in my hands wrapped in tissue. I savored the cake, which was dripping in chocolate sauce, it was my first desert in over a year.

"We miss you so much, your cooking, your laughter, the songs on the way to school, the house is miserable without you, Mum misses you, she's just afraid to show it, and Dad shows no emotion which is nothing new!" James began.

"I miss you all, I hope I will escape!" I sighed.

Suddenly a dark shadow clouded over me, it was sister Elizabeth, scowling, and looking on disgusted, grabbing the cake cruelly and throwing it onto the floor.

"You fucking bitch!" Mena yelled.

Sister Elizabeth looked on, her jaw dropped, seeing that someone would dare answer her back, as I watched them walk away, I looked on in shock as Sister Elizabeth collapsed on the floor, she looked exacerbated, maybe in that moment she knew the depth of her cruelty, she would have to have been blind not to notice her malice.

That evening I spent time with the girls, in the dormitory, talking about the future and singing songs together.

Anita massaged cream into my hair that had been sneaked in by her school friend.

"What do you want to do when you leave the laundry?"

"I'd love to be a social worker, and help children and adults going through hardship, I will work in a local bar and then attend night school, you are never too old to chase your dreams Eileen, what are your dreams?"

"I want to work as a staff nurse, and run my own ward, seeing new people, and having a new work routine, and living in a little town house in Dublin with my bulldog Ben, no rules, no expectations, and just to be free!"

"You will get your life of freedom, just make sure that next time you escape you don't get caught!" Anita warned.

I felt like Anita was one of my older sister's, she was always there when I felt alone, and offered advice, there was no time to make friends in the asylum, friendships were not permitted, we were watched like a hawk by the nun's, and were only permitted to talk in the courtyard, and even then each interaction was monitored.

I spent the next part of the evening helping Bernadette to peel her orange, she looked up at me and mouthed, 'Christmas,' I was happy that she was able to understand, I sat and brushed her hair and platted it, she felt relaxed around me, and I felt a sense of responsibility towards her.

Then I lay on the bed with Lucy as she flicked through her Elvis picture book.

"Do you think I'll be able to travel to America, to see Elvis in his show?"

"When we leave here, we will both get jobs, work long hours and we'll go together, there is so much for us to experience!" I cheered.

Despite being in hell, and almost turning
seventeen, I had a day of escapism, which is what
I needed, after being treated like a slave all year.

Then a group of young children stood by the steel
gates outside, dressed in white singing, 'Hark the
herald angels singing,' we all knelt below the
window and joined in with the chorus, it was the
most perfect moment, we were connected as a
group.

Chapter 5: Easter Parade

I will never forget the night of the fire, Bernadette was coughing profusely, and Anita grabbed my arms, trying desperately to wake me up. Smoke filled up the room, and we could hear the screams of the other girls in the dormitory. The nun's hurried in such a panic, for once all almighty and powerful Sister Elizabeth looked terrified and scared.

"Quick, girls, exit the room immediately and follow me!" She warned. We followed the Elizabeth to the door at the end of the corridor the fire exit, the door which we were forbidden to enter. We were terrified as we ran down the spiral staircase with sheets, covering us, holding them over our heads trying to conceal the smoke.

We made our way to the courtyard, and watched, in awe, as the building erupted into magnificent flames, many of the girl's cheered but I remained silent, confused, and scared of what was to happen next. Many of the girl's believed the fire was arson from a previous survivor of the asylum, but the culprit was never found.

We then stayed in a cold abandoned warehouse, and we slept in a giant room, together, and slept on blow up beds, whilst one month of refurbishments started on the asylum. I remember a local library gave us unlimited books to read, I must have read every series by Charles Dicken's. We were so happy to be away from the laundry, it was like respite, but like all good things it was too good to be true, we returned after a month to a life of hard work.

A week after we returned it was time for the Easter parade. I detested the Easter parade immensely, we wore blue, and we had to attend mass in the church courtyard with all our families and the local town present. I detested how we were presented as young women who were cared for by the nun's, I wanted to scream out, I wanted to tell the truth about the abuse inflicted.

On the day of the parade as we walked up to our seats in the courtyard, I felt my whole-body shake, my siblings waved to me, but my parents quickly gave them a stern look, warning them to divert their attention. I was not aware that events were about to take a turn for the worse really fast.

After the mass, Mena crept towards me as I sat at the edge of the row, and she embraced me tightly, before looking on in horror at the bruises on my arms.

"Why have you got so many bruises on your arms? who did this?" she yelled.

"Mena please, don't worry, please," I begged.

I watched as Mena's face turned red with rage, she dropped to the ground, grabbing a pile of mud in her hand, and charged towards Sister Elizabeth, grabbing her, and smearing the mud over her face.

"You are a complete animal, leave Eileen alone, if you touch her again, I'll come for you!" she yelled. I watched as Sister Elizabeth stood, frozen, whilst my mother grabbed her and pulled her back.

All eyes were on Mena, and we were all quickly hurried from the scene, I still remember seeing Mena's face as I looked back, full of rage, crying, she was so worried about me.

I wondered what Mena's punishment would be, how my parents would react, I knew she could not control her temper.

The day after, Sister Elizabeth ordered me to clean the floors of the hallway, and she came towards me, and she stood on my hand, and I let out a deafening scream, I knew this was her

revenge, I paid the price for my sister's outburst.

With each punishment my humanity slipped away.

Chapter 6: Time moves on.

A year had passed so slowly, and here I was at 18

years of age, a grown adult, thinking of my peers

at school, moving on to Jobs, enjoying their first relationships, making their first steps towards adulthood.

I had become immune to the slavery subjected to me at a cost. I now had juvenile arthritis, my hands were red and cracked, my back was in pain, and I began to get varicose veins. It was clear that working in the laundry was having a physical impact on me.

I had noticed that Anita had grown more weaker, and would sometimes have to be excused in completing duties, due to extreme tiredness and weakness.

Bernadette's behavior had worsened she had been screaming involuntarily, and she would swear whenever the nuns would come close, and I worked so hard to help her remain calm, stroking her hair, and begging the Nun's to not hit her. I hoped there was a doctor to assess both Anita and Bernadette, but they were never introduced.

Across the way from the laundry the abandoned warehouse had been converted into a Children's home for the children of the Magdalene women. I remember first peering from the window and observing the children, all dressed in ragged white clothes, their faces were pale, and they had bags under their eyes, they looked malnourished, impoverished and frightened. I thought about John, trying to imagine what my son would look like aged two, if he was walking, if he was saying his first words, it was a weird feeling of strong unreciprocated love.

I had not given up wanting to escape the laundry, I was mentally stronger than before, and became fearless, willing to face the consequences, but more confident that I could escape the clutches of the guards.

Lucy got me through the darkest times in the laundry, at night we would lay together on the bed, telling each other ghost stories, singing Elvis's songs, and even star gazing into the early hours of the morning. For every unpleasant situation in life there is always a way you can turn it around into a positive.

Two new nuns were introduced into the Laundry, both in their early twenties, and they were both polar opposites. Maria was twenty and kind, and gentle, and would offer sandwiches and sweets to the girls behind the backs of the other nuns. It felt great to finally have someone looking out for us. Then there was Julia, an angry and vicious 21-year-old nun, a mini-Sister Elizabeth, who was stern in every task, and introduced room spot checks.

I woke up on 1st August, the sun was beating down and I could feel the hot sun cast a shadow over my face in the morning. I knew it was going to be a tough day in the laundry, it always was with the hot weather. I wrapped a blanket over Anita who was shivering with a cold. I could see that her skin was pale, and her lips were mottled. I helped to sit her up to give her a refreshing glass of water.

"Where is the pain today, Anita?"

"Everywhere, I slept poorly all night, I have been exhausted, hold my hand for a while," She pleaded.

I did not feel much comfort, seeing her in so much pain, I only took contentment that she was taking her medications that was helping her pain, I struggled to release grip of her hand, just as I did every morning.

That morning I began the work duty, sweating, my back ached as I swirled the filthy laundry around the basin, the clothes were thick with mud and grease. As I stood on the step ladder, I admired the robins and the bluebirds, and the robins sang in the oak trees, it was so soothing.

A new girl Agatha was making trouble in the laundry. I could see that she was rough and ready, and unwilling to listen to orders, she was complaining that the water was too hot and was shouting obscenities to the nuns. Then she began to sway the basin from side to side before tipping the water all over the floor. I knew inside that the girls were laughing inside, along with me, glad that a girl had managed to stand up for her beliefs. I watched as she stormed away before the guards grabbed her down the hallway into the basement. It took some girl's longer to come to terms with being a prisoner in the asylum, and it took some people longer to fit in, to avoid the terrible stigma they faced.

Just before the end of the working day as I went to the toilet I could hear a voice, whispering, it was Lucy.

"Come on Eileen, come outside quick!"

"We can't! it's uniform check soon!" I yelled.

Lucy took me by the hand dragged me out of the back door, and I looked out in wonder as the mermaid fountain which had been broken had now turned on. I danced with Lucy around in a circle, the water felt so refreshing on one of the hottest days of the year. Above us was a beautiful rainbow shining over us, it was the most beautiful experience to feel free and happy.

Suddenly we heard the door open, and we hid around the corner.

"Is there anyone out there?" Maria yelled in a soft accent.

Then she found us and smiled sweetly guiding us through the back gate, and we ran quickly up the stairs and dried off in the bathroom.

After I walked out of the bathroom, I walked to the window and saw the brightest rainbow still shining across the cornfield, I took it as a sign that things were about to change, and that luck was coming my way.

I then turned to Anita, and my heart sank, Anita's face was deathly pale, and her arms were stretched out on the bed. I knelt onto the wooden floor and leaned my head towards her face, and checked her pulse on her wrist. I could see that she had died.

It was an incredible shock, the one person who I had looked up to every day, and turned to for some advice, a mother to me was gone. I tried to contain my emotion, but erupted into a flood of tears, as the other girls stood around the bed in shock gasping.

Soon Sister Elizabeth and Louisa dragged me away from the bed. I began to shout in rage, "You never listened to me! You never gave her the help she needed," I screamed.

I had seen how sick Anita had become, and begged for her to be sent to hospital, her skin was mottled, and there were times I would look at her and see that her skin was dry, she would go in and out of consciousness.

I collapsed into the corner and fell to the floor, I then watched in horror as the ambulance team arrived. They completed observations and completed CPR, but it was no good, she was pronounced dead at 8pm. I felt so lost, Anita represented strength to me, and I knew that her absence would leave a huge gap in my life.

Later that night, I walked up to Anita's bed, I could see that her name was etched on the wall, I opened the floorboard from underneath her bed and observed her hidden box. I walked over to my bed and silently opened the box. I found a hairbrush, a photo of Anita at the prom in a beautiful white dress, and her diary filled with affirmations, and positive words, which helped her to carry on during her darkest times. I held the white sheet over me and began to silently cry, as the cool breeze brushed past my skin I clenched my fists tightly, I knew I had to be strong, I knew that was what Anita would want, and I was determined more than ever to escape and leave the laundry.

Time moved on so slowly, the grief of losing Anita came in waves, I would cry thinking about her night, or suddenly I would think about her whilst completing laundry, but there was no one to talk to, no counseling service, I had to cope on my own.

I looked in the mirror, three years after entering the laundry, and I saw a worn-out depressed person, a girl who had severe backpain, aching feet, and deep varicose veins, which impaired my ability to walk, leading to constant pain.

As expected, a new girl arrived, Kayleigh, a sixteen-year-old girl accused of pushing her stepmother down the stairs, even though she protested that it was a suicide attempt by her wicked stepmother.

After the first day of work, I observed Kayleigh sitting up in the bed, shivering, her face flushed, and struggling to sleep after a day of hard labor.

"Oh, Kayleigh how are you? I know the first day is tough, but we are all here for you."

"Why is this allowed? How can women work here all day without any pay? If it was men instead of women they would be paid, and all that is left for us is a soggy dinner and warm water, it's inhumane."

"We will get you through this, nothing is forever!"
I smiled as I embraced her. As I looked back at
my reflection in the cracked mirror I could see the
dark circles under my eyes, I felt like I was taking
over the role of Anita as the mother figure. Then
the fear ran over me, I did not want to die in the
laundry, I needed my life back before it was too
late.

The age of 19, felt like such a pivotal age, my
mother gave birth to me at 19, many of my
friends were engaged to be married, life was
moving so fast, and I felt left behind.

Mal and Dom were now at school, Mena was
engaged to be married, Minnie was planning on

moving at the end of the year, and James had started an apprentice as a builder. I felt like I was trapped in a bubble, and I was desperately lonely and then a miracle happened.

It was now October, and we experienced the worst snow fall I had ever witnessed. The snow was over ten feet high, covering the fields. It was so peaceful in the morning, a stark contrast to the heavy drizzle of rain which we constantly experienced. I looked out of the window, and took comfort in seeing the robins perching on the tree, and the morning fog felt refreshing against my skin, as I opened the window to take in the cold air.

I was unaware that a miracle was about to happen, and it was so easy and required no effort by me. Sister Elizabeth had punished me and Lucy for talking, and we were sent out to the corridor to clean the floor with the ragged cloth.

Then we watched as Sister Elizabeth stomped through in her muddy boots, causing more dirt, and then the miracle occurred, the spare keys fell from her pocket onto the floor, and I quickly grabbed them, concealing them in my pocket, Lucy looked on in wonder.

"Are we going to do it? This is a sign that we need to go, and we need to go quickly!"

"Well, I'm not going to die here like Anita, we will get out Friday night, it's a quiet night and gives us the best chance," I promised.

I observed sister Elizabeth's wicked expression, and I was more determined than ever to enact revenge.

I sat on a rock on Bundoran beach and watched as a family ran along the beach, a little girl in a red dress holding a blue kite, she looked so free and content.

Although I was feeling so ill, I felt so at peace at the beach, listening to the waves crash, and the seagulls swooping above me.

I could see my 15-year-old self-diving into the sea, whilst Minnie was burying Mal and Dom in the sand, and my parents and other siblings were sitting on the bench, singing and enjoying ice creams together.

Now that I am older, I miss the memories of being an innocent child, after I went to the laundry, I had the stigma placed on me as the fallen girl that never went away, I felt like I was living in a snow globe, trying to trap myself in the perfect memory of my life.

Chapter 7: The Escape

I had spent a week in the laundry with Lucy plotting to escape, and I had not envisioned how seriously she had taken it. Lucy had stolen a rope, from the guard's room, to help us climb over the wall if we struggled to get out of the gate. I also discovered that Lucy had firecrackers as ammunition, a bottle of water, and a bag of rocks to throw at the guards if they attack us. We had planned to get our belongings together at 11pm, an hour after lights out, giving us enough time to leave safely. I was going to miss Bernadette she was so vulnerable, constantly crying, her body was covered in scratches, and she struggled to sleep each night. I wondered how she would cope without me, I was the only one she would listen to, the only person she felt comfortable with, but I knew I could not take her with me, she was far too weak, physically and emotionally, and far too unstable to cope with the escape plan.

The final day was one of mixed feelings, I made sure I was well rested and refreshed to have the energy to escape. It was a day of final events, the final day I would eat cold and lumpy porridge, my hands ached terribly, as I cleaned the laundry in the huge basin, riddled with arthritis and aching in pain. I watched as Lucy attempted to push her luck, talking to other girls' and taking her time to complete tasks, she was becoming carefree, but I knew I had to remain compliant until the very end.

The night time seemed to last forever; we both lay together on the bed contemplating the future.

"What do you want to do once you leave?" Lucy asked.

"Well, I've missed out on three years of my life, there is so much I want to do. I want to finish school, attend night school and eventually study to become a nurse. I have spent so long caring for Bernadette, and helping others in the asylum, I feel I was meant to help others, and I know I can achieve it, and becoming financially independent. What do you intend to do?" I asked.

"Work in Dublin, as a hairdresser for a while, in the future I want to work in performing arts, but I don't care as long as we are free, we have to stick together!" Lucy pondered.

"When we escape, I want us to go to my house before we leave for Dublin, if we reach my house at 7am James will be ready for work, and we can take a ride to the train station on the two-seater basket on the end of his bike."

"I hope the plan works!" Lucy begged.

"It will it has to!" I assured.

As we lay in the bed, I tried to relax as the crickets sang in the background. At 11pm, I watched as Lucy stood up grabbing the bag of rocks and firecrackers. I was petrified, inside, but knew that the plan had to go ahead it was now or never.

We tiptoed out of the dormitory, and held onto the banister as we quickly made our way down the creaky, rotten, staircase. I was shaking already, although we had only started our journey.

As we made our way to the bottom of the stairs, we ran to the front entrance, I could feel my hand trembling as I quickly unlocked the front door, and we hurried to the front gate using the master key to unlock the steel spiked gate. I took off my black pumps and ran bare foot, holding onto Lucy's hand, stepping on glass but suffering the pain if we were to be chased by the guards.

It was the most beautiful clear night, with the full moon shining on us, and the breeze brushing past us, as we made our way to the forest.

"What are we going to do? They will come looking for us!" Lucy questioned.

"We will carry on, we will find a hiding place, and then at 6am, we will make our way to my house," I assured her.

We walked for over an hour through the forest, until we found a dug out covered my branches, we climbed inside and hid, I collected branches to enable Lucy to rest her head whilst I kept a look out.

My head was filled in pain, and my heart was still racing, my feet ached and bled from the glass and the rocks. I picked the glass out before wrapping both of my feet in bandages. I could not focus, convinced that the guards were going to find us, I was amazed they had not found us sooner.

Lucy fell into a deep sleep, she fell into a state of exhaustion, and I must have soaked myself in water from the bottle, I had never been so thirsty.

Moments later, I was met by the most beautiful deer, with big glowing brown eyes, she stared at me with confusion, I reached out my hand and she disappeared. I thought about my family wondering if my parents would ever accept my apology, or if I would have to run away to Dublin with Lucy, with no plan, no money, I was so worried about the future.

Then I thought about my son, knowing that now he was three, he would be ready for nursery, I imagined that he had thick curly blonde hair and sea blue eyes like me, and that he enjoyed playing sports, but I knew this was all in my imagination. I then wondered if he would ever try and find me, I hoped that I would be financially stable, and wondered if I would be able to have a family of my own one day.

I fought so hard to stay awake, despite the fear and anxiety, I lost the battle and collapsed into a deep slumber.

I awoke the next morning, at 5am, to a light drizzle, as I looked out the branches had been removed, and Lucy was standing there with her satchel.

"Come on we have to go; we only have an hour!" Lucy began.

As we made our way, through the rustled leaves and the branches, I struggled to walk on my injured feet, as Lucy held onto my shoulder.

"We will never make it to your home in an hour, maybe we should rest for a while, until you get stronger." Lucy offered.

It was then that a milk truck appeared, parking up on the side of the road.

"We will hitch a ride!" Lucy beamed.

"No, we can't trust anyone, he may take us back to the asylum." I warned.

Lucy ran up to the young, startled, milkman and hugged him.

"Oh sir I was wondering if you could help me we need to get to Dalston avenue, we know it's on the way, but we need complete secrecy, we are escaping from the laundry, if anyone stops you, and asks about our whereabouts keep it secret." Lucy warned.

"I am a sucker for two beautiful girls, this one time only though!" He smiled.

As we climbed into the back of the milk man, the man put a blanket around us whilst giving us a glass of milk each. We were both so thirsty that we poured the refreshing cold milk over our faces, we were only use to stale and warm milk in the asylum.

It felt great to be free, as we listened to the sounds of the blue birds chirping, but disaster struck. A car behind us beeped the horn at the van, and we shook as it halted.

I could hear the heavy footprints of the boots, that familiar sound of the guards.

"Excuse me Sir, we are looking for two girls' over five foot four, who have escaped the laundry, one with blonde hair, one with black curly hair. They are a danger to the community."

I felt sick as I squeezed tightly onto Lucy's hand, as we froze and remained as still as we could.

"No sir, I have not seen anyone, just the usual farmyard animals, but I will keep a look out."

 I felt the flash of the torch from the guard, as he guided his touch around the back of the van, and then disappeared.

As we continued along the road, Lucy appeared to burst with excitement, and jumped up.

"We've escaped the clutches of the laundry, we're finally free!" Lucy cheered.

"We are not out of the woods yet, we still need to keep a low profile, they may be at the train station waiting, we will need to take my sister's hats, we need a disguise, we can't go back there, we may never get out!" I warned.

We arrived at Dalston Avenue at 6:10am, and we jumped out of the milk van, and we stood on the cobbled road.

I cried as I looked at my beautiful thatched cottage, with the blue door, I could smell the fried bacon and eggs from the kitchen, we hid, just as my Father left on his bike to work, I was thankful in a way, terrified of his reaction, and possible reaction to me.

I slowly opened the door, and sitting at the table was Mal and Dom, with Mena, whilst James was standing by the stove.

Mal, Dom, and Mena embraced me tightly, whilst James looked concerned.

"Eileen it is great to have you home, please don't leave us again!" Mal ordered.

"We need to get you both hidden before Mummy wakes up, and then we can decide on a plan," Mena offered.

"What happened? How did you escape? Ma and Pa will not have you stay here, what are you going to do?" James warned.

"We are travelling to Dublin, we were hoping you could take us to the station on your bike," I began.

"Dublin? How can you go to Dublin with no money no job, it won't work," James panicked.

"We will find a way," I promised.

It was then that my blood went cold, I could hear my mother calling the guards from the conservatory, before coming into the kitchen crying hysterically in her blue nightgown.

"Mum how could you?" James shouted.

"Right let's go!" James offered.

We ran outside and jumped into the seats at the back of the bike, it was then that Mena arrived with a plastic bag, filled with two dresses and hats, I knew she could tell what I was thinking.

I had never seen James ride the bike so fast, as I turned around, I could see my mother's distraught, red blotchy face, I wondered why she had betrayed me, what did I do to deserve this?

"We will hide in the station toilet, and change into our outfits, we just have to find a suitable hiding place on the train." I began.

It was then that Lucy took out money from her pocket.

"I stole it from the nun's dressing room, yesterday, I have been resourceful since you have found the keys."

At 7am, we arrived at the train station, and as we jumped off the bike, I emotionally embraced James, before he put money in an envelope and gave it to me.

"This should tide you over for a while, keep in touch when it's safe, I wish you both all the luck!" He smiled.

I watched him ride into the distance, wondering when I would ever see him again.

I hurried with Lucy into the changing cubicles as we put on the dresses and wide brimmed hats. For three years we were kept locked up in the laundry, and this felt daring, adventurous, we were nervous for our new life.

As we stepped out, we looked on the noticeboard, observing that we had only five minutes until the train to Dublin arrived.

We sat at the bench, both waiting nervously for the train.

"The disguises were a great idea; I can't believe we've finally made it! When we are in Dublin we will get jobs as waitresses, find a place to rent, we will be free!" Lucy beamed.

"I recognize that voice!" Shouted the guard, before he grabbed Lucy forcefully by the arm. I watched as Lucy put her hand around her back, grabbed the rock, and hit him on the head knocking him back.

The train arrived, and just as the doors opened, we saw another guard in the distance, charging towards us. We got on the train and the doors closed on the furious guards, who banged on the doors to no avail, as the final whistle blew.

We sat in the carriage and tried to relax, I held onto my chest hoping for my heart to calm down. We embraced each other and burst into tears.

"We made it!" Lucy cheered, jumping up and down from her seat.

I rested back on the chair, feeling mixed emotions, I had been abandoned by my mother, but I was free from a life of misery and imprisonment in the laundry, and I now knew the true meaning of freedom.

Chapter 8: Welcome to Dublin

We arrived at Dublin at 5pm, to the bright lights of the city, the noise of the cars shooting past, and glamorous people walking past.

Immediately as we walked down the cobbled street, I felt suspicious of the people passing by, I pulled my hat lower, believing that people were looking at me, 'the fallen girl' 'the criminal' it was a stigma I was soon to discover would never leave.

Our first stop was St Michael's bakery where we stopped for a cup of mint tea and a slice of fruit cake. We stood out, in our oversized outfits, we were so hungry, we consumed the cake in seconds. We thought about the girls in the asylum, and thought about the laundry tasks we would be completing, if we were still at the asylum.

"Where are we going to stay? We need a plan if we are going to survive here?" I asked.

"Well, we've got enough money from your brother to stay at a hotel tonight, and I have a friend who works at a hairdressers' nearby she may be able to hold us up, whilst we save up for a place of our own." Lucy added.

I was apprehensive, knowing that Lucy was an overly optimistic person, and I could not rely on her for a solid plan.

After the café, we made our way to the picture house to watch an Elvis film. I bought a bucket of popcorn, whilst Lucy bought the Pepsi colas.

Throughout the film we sang along to the songs, and popcorn flew into the air in excitement, we were constantly hungry all the time, it was as if we were making up for the poor diet in the asylum. We were lost in our own world; we could not see the disruption we were causing at the usher politely ordered us to leave the auditorium.

Then the most amazing thing happened, a mysterious woman in a red coat, with her curly hair wrapped in a ball, grabbed us both by the shoulder.

"I heard you both talking about being in the laundry, my sister was there and released two years ago. I could not help hearing that you are both struggling and have money worries. You are both very welcome to stay at my apartment this weekend, I would really love to help," Jenny smiled.

Jenny walked us to her beautiful apartment with a black and white television, a cream king size sofa, and the guest rooms had two king size beds with velvet sheets, the view from the room was of Dublin city, we were both very fortunate that Jenny supported us, and we admired her wonderful act of human kindness.

We enjoyed a banquet of lasagna, an assortment of fruit, and a refreshing glass of lemonade, we were both so hungry, it was so wonderful to have warm food, we had longed for a warm meal. Before we went to bed, that night, we enjoyed a warm shower. I felt like I was in heaven with fresh shower gel, when we had struggle with a rotten bar of soap, and freezing cold water for so long.

After staying at Jenny's apartment, we decided that we were going to use my brother's money to stay at a hotel.

The Radisson hotel was basic but comfortable, we had two double beds a small television and a tray of biscuits. Lucy was like a Duracell bunny, jumping up and down the bed, whilst I was so tired, I had missed out on so much rest in the asylum, and it was a luxury to have my own bed.

I had tried to remain positive, but the feelings of abandonment crept over me, I had a romanticized view when I left the asylum, that my family would accept me back, and my life would go back to normal. It was much harder to start on my own, I had no financial backing, little emotional support, and the loneliness which consumed me each day, in the asylum, bore within me in Dublin.

The following morning, we went down to the breakfast bar, we filled our plates up with hash browns, mash, sausages, and slices of toast. I laughed at how fast Lucy was eating, I consumed three glasses of orange juice. It was a novelty to have a cold refreshing drink, and a novelty to have choice of food, a human right.

After breakfast, Lucy took us to her friend Michelle's hairdresser 'clipper's'

Michelle wore a bright orange dress and looked like an orange, her face full of make up, and she was very pleased to see us. I was in awe as she took us to the office, offering us both a part time job imminently, and a place to stay in her apartment upstairs. The apartment was cramped, and filled with boxes, but we were glad that we had a place to stay.

Working in the hairdressers was not very stimulating, and much of our time was taken up, sweeping hair from the floor, or washing people's hair or making tea. I needed to expand my mind and help people, to have a purpose in life. The final straw came when Mrs. Evan's smashed her tea on the floor complaining that it was too cold.

I applied to the local nursing college, and as I submitted my nursing application, I was in tears writing it. I had achieved great grades at school, my record was exemplary, I found it difficult documenting my three-year absence at the laundry, instantly thinking I would be rejected.

A week later, I was ecstatic to receive a call to come to the office of Nurse Clark, to discuss my application.

I was so nervous as I made my way to the meeting convinced, I was about to receive a rejection.

Nurse Clark was welcoming, with her warm smile, sitting with a fresh pot of tea.

"I didn't make it, you don't want me on the course," I began.

"Quite the contrary Eileen, your grades are above average, your application was well presented, we would love for you to start with us next week." Nurse Clark began.

"Oh really, I can't thank you enough, this is my dream, I thought because of my past I would be rejected. I am so thankful you have given me a chance."

"Well, everyone deserves a chance, and we do not judge here, you gained a place on this course by your own merit, and we feel you would be an asset to the team," Nurse Clarke beamed.

I was elated and overjoyed, finally feeling like I had achieved something, and that I had a sense of purpose.

When I arrived back at the apartment, I could see that Lucy was taking a wild approach to her newfound freedom, despite my many pleas, she was constantly out partying, making new friends, and drinking heavily. I felt so sorry for Lucy, she was so vulnerable, her father abandoned her as a small child, whilst her mother raised her on her low wage as a receptionist. I was trying to help her, and at the time I did not see the warning signs of how desperately she was in need of

direction.

I was so excited to start nursing school, I stood in front of the long mirror looking on in awe at my white uniform, with my fob watch. I felt like my dream was coming true, but I also felt like a fraud, the nuns in the asylum made us feel like we could achieve anything.

Before I left the house, I went into Lucy's room to find her crashed out on the bed, in a drunken stupor. I helped to reposition her in the bed and placed the covers over her gently, she was trying to escape the world, and was already given a final warning at work, but I had to get on with my own life.

I arrived at the nursing school to find all of the girl's sitting in the cold clinical classroom, all in their pristine white unform and eager to learn. Then I saw her my ex-school colleague, Sophie, the school bully, sitting in the center of the room. Sophie knew my secret, she knew I was a Magdalene girl, and I knew she was about to blow my secret.

We sat at the table with the strict nurse instructor Helen, Helen was built like a bull, and was six foot tall and over twenty stone, and would walk around the classroom, waving her stick around, striking the fear of God into the girl's.

In the first clinical session we each had an orange on our desk, with a syringe, to practice our injection technique. Helen made me complete the technique over ten times until I got it right. .

Then we had to complete our bandaging technique, ensuring that the bandages were completed with care and accuracy. I met a seventeen-year-old girl called Anna, straight out of school, I lied to her telling her that I worked as a waitress for two years as a career break, It felt great to be around other people, I felt damaged and I wanted to shake the criminal image.

Just as I was about to leave the classroom, Sophie came towards me and forcefully embraced me.

"Oh, Eileen it is so wonderful to see you, how have the past two years in the Magdalene home been for you?" She scowled loudly.

I watched as the other nursing students stopped in their tracks, looking at me in shock, and Anna looked at me confused.

I felt humiliated and ran out of the building in tears, I felt like I was still a prisoner, trapped in the world of the asylum.

Then as I arrived home, I felt a note on the kitchen table 'Lucy sent to hospital.'

I began to panic as I made my way to the hospital, to find Lucy attached to a drip, her face pale, and as she saw me, she began to cry.

"What happened?" I asked.

"I felt extremely sick, around midday today, I called the ambulance and when they arrived, I was barely conscious. They say I have alcohol poisoning and they have warned me from alcohol."

"We need to start afresh, from now on we can't let the trauma of what we've been through bring us down, carry on with your hairdressing, I'll carry on with my nursing course, we need to sleep, go for walk's and spend less time alone," I smiled, trying to mask the pain.

I held onto Lucy's hand; we were both broken, broken pieces waiting to be put together again.

Our new life in Dublin felt like a fresh start, but the past was haunting us.

Chapter 9: Rebuilding life.

Lucy finally was discharged from hospital two weeks later, after being warned that if she drank anymore, she was risking permanent damage to her lungs. I spent evenings supporting her as she spent time in bed, encouraging her to drink fluids and cooking her meals.

Then one evening I received a knock on the door it was Mena, James, Mal and Dom, they had travelled to see me unknown to my mother who believed they were staying with my cousins. It felt so wonderful having them with me after a three-year absence, they brought along sleeping bags, cookies, and a monopoly boardgame.

James treated us to a movie night at the cinema where we watched 'It's a wonderful life' Mal and Dom ran around the aisles, whilst James fell asleep, and me and Mena watched the film in tears.

When we arrived home, Mena sat with me in the kitchen and gave me an envelope of photos of a baby boy, my son John.

"Where did you get these pictures?"

"I tracked him down from my friend Bertie who works at the adoption agency, he lives in London now with his adoptive parents, they are American and both doctor's."

I observed the black and white photos of John, and I began to cry. There was not a day that passed where I did not think of him, I could see that he resembled me, almost identical in baby photos of me as a child.

"Do you think you will ever fight to get him back?" Mena asked.

"I can't he has a wonderful life and the financial security I could never give him, with two successful parents, maybe if he wants to find me one day I would accept that, I think about him every day, becoming a nurse helps me to have a focus, and forget the trauma."

I held onto the photos, now making it more poignant and harder now that I could visually see what my child looked like.

Mena was now successful and a qualified pharmacist, and due to be married the following December, Mal and Dom were both at school, and James was a successful electrician, so much had changed and moved forward.

"Eileen, I want you to be my bridesmaid in December, will you?" Mena asked.

"What about Mum and Dad? They won't allow me to go to the wedding."

"You're an adult, I'm inviting you, I won't let you carry on being punished," Mena smiled.

That night as my siblings slept in the room with me, it felt like I was at home again, life almost felt normal again, but I knew I would not achieve this until I gained the forgiveness from my parents.

I watched my siblings walk off into the distance towards the station, and I was thankful they were back in my life.

As I went back into the house I sat at the table and looked at the

black and white photos of my son. I began to cry, thinking of all the milestones I missed out on, his firsts steps, first words, watching him experience the word through the time. I felt a sense of sadness, knowing that his parents were doctors, and they were able to give him the life I could

never give him, the perfect education, holidays,

and stability of a loving family. I put the photos

back in the draw, trying not to look at them,

trying to put the situation in the past.

I arrived at the hospital at 8am for my first shift

as a student nurse, I was incredibly nervous, I

had heard all the stories about the strict

environments, the angry matrons, and the need for perfection in every task.

I arrived on the ward to meet Nurse Diane, a kindhearted nurse who knew the name of each patient, and provided person centered care to each patient.

I looked around the ward, anxious and scared, I observed the male patients and one female patient.

The first patient was Michael, a sixty-year-old man, admitted with shortness of breath and was breathing with the assistance of an oxygen mask, on his bedside table were two empty whiskey bottles.

The second patient was Thomas, aged 80, admitted with influenza, he sat in his bed surrounded by tissues, sneezing everywhere.

The third patient was Jeffrey, aged 71, admitted with gallstones and complained about the pains he felt, holding onto his stomach in anger.

In the next bed was Helen, a sixty-five-year-old lady admitted with confusion and would sing 'Vera Lynne's 'we'll meet again' constantly.

I felt like a lamb to the slaughter on my first day, everything was brand new to me and I felt so clumsy, my hands began to shake uncontrollably, with nerves, and fear of making a mistake.

We completed the morning washes, carrying the huge grey silver basins to patients, washing them behind the old ragged blue curtains. We washed Jeffrey who immediately lost the use of his hands when we began to wash him, and he had a big smile on his face.

"Well, my darling girl's, I'm in heaven, being washed by two wonderful nurses like you, life does not get any better!" he smiled. After the wash we assisted Jeffrey into his orange pajama's which made every patient look like a prisoner.

"Get me a urine bottle!" He urged.

I ran to the waste cupboard where all the hospital supplies were kept, and ran back with the urine bottle. After Jeffrey used the bottle, I took it from his hands and in my nervous state I poured it all over my trousers.

Sister Diana guided me to the changing room, giving me a spare set of clothes, a huge blue nurse top and baggy trousers, which made me resemble a clown.

We then supported Helen who immediately felt confused in my presence as she looked at nurse Diane.

"Who is this child? Why is she here? So gormless and pale," She began.

"This is Eileen a student nurse, she is here to help you today."

"A slip of a girl like her, oh Diane I hate children, especially chubby ones!" she yelled.

As we moved on from the disastrous first interaction, Helen consented to the wash, although she was still acutely confused. Helen was suffering from delirium, due to poor nutrition and lack of fluids, we had to gently encourage her to drink.

After the wash, Helen agreed for me brush her hair. Then as I walked away, she threw her brush at me and grabbed the bowl of water drenching me from head to toe, I felt like my first shift was going terribly, my nerves seem to get the better of me.

I watched Diana and how intricately she completed each task, carefully ensuring each patient had their medications, that each patient had an adequate meal to eat. I admired her natural ability to cheer patients up with laughter, singing, and listening to their stories, boosting their morale in a hostile environment.

Then during the night, we could hear the banging of the heels of the matron Kate coming up the corridor.

Kate came into the ward like a bull, and the other nurses and orderlies stood by the beds in military style as she checked the state the wards.

Then in common fashion for that time, matron Kate ordered me, a lowly student to give her a report of each patient, she wanted to know their condition, prognosis, and treatment plan.

I don't know how I managed to, but I was able to adequately give a report of each patient.

The rest of the night was filled with drama at each turn, I had to watch Helen who became increasingly confused by the hour, running around the ward, singing loudly, keeping the other patients awake, and pouring water over the other nurses. Then I had to attend to the buzzer constantly being pressed by Michael for the simplest of tasks, helping him to sit up in the bed, or helping him to drink his glass of water. Nursing at times felt like being a maid, we had to complete and attend to every whim and request of each patient. I was so thankful for Diane's support, she was almost like a mother figure, she was there to support me emotionally, and would often give me bonuses in my pay packet each

month to tide me over.

Chapter 10: Lucy

A year had now passed, I was twenty-one and was still very junior in my role as nurse, although a lot was expected of nurses, including managing entire wards and responding to emergencies, and trying to cope with limited resources to handle complex situations.

Mena's wedding was extremely hard to get through, my parents refused to talk to me and looked at me as if I was an outcast. My father looked so much older and frail, he had psoriasis of the liver due to his excessive drinking, I was devastated a month later when he passed away from his condition. I was distraught that despite this, my mother continued to ignore me and treat me like a criminal.

I had come to the realization that I would pay the price for having a child out of wedlock my whole life, meaning that romantic relationships and friendships would be hard due to a lack of trust. I did not realize at the time, I was suffering with post traumatic stress, struggling to sleep, having panic attacks, and awful nightmares of being trapped in the attic of the asylum, but there was no help or support on offer.

Lucy was improving in her own mental health, she was now a nursery teacher, and had met a man called Derek and was engaged to be married, though she planned to stay with me until the wedding. Lucy had completely stopped drinking and her moods were stable, her complexion improved, and she was making clear choices, I was so happy that she was coping, especially as her family, who abandoned her had now moved to America.

On my 21st birthday, I received a card from Mena which left me shaken, confused and down a dangerous path. Mena had enclosed a picture of my five-year-old son in his blue uniform, he had wild curly hair and bright blue eyes, he looked just like my brother James. Then as I looked at the back of the photograph, I was left shaken as she had enclosed the address of his home in central London, and the name of his school.

For months I kept the photo in the draw, but I could not stop thinking about the address, knowing that I could find my son, and I made the disastrous decision to visit London.

I was young, with no guidance, and made the choice out of loneliness and a feeling of wanting to gain closure.

I travelled on the ferry to London, wearing a long black jacket, hat, and huge black sunglasses, to disguise myself throughout my London visit.

I found London so overwhelming, everyone was rushing past, no one would stop to help with directions. The men wore smart suits, whilst the women wore beautiful dresses with fur and mink coats.

On the first day in London, I tried to distract myself drinking in the Blake coffee house, as I sat outside, people smiled at me, here I could escape the image of the lost Magdalene girl, I could be anyone, and I loved the idea of anonymity. I stayed at the holiday express hotel, exhausted, I slept like a log.

The following morning it was the most beautiful sunny morning, after I consumed the English breakfast with fresh juice, I made my way, about to conduct my dangerous plan.

At midday, I made my way to St Micheal's Nursery I watched as the children ran out at lunchtime. I watched carefully and after five minutes I saw my son John. My whole body felt completely numb, he was running around playing with a ball, I wanted to shout 'my son' I wanted to go over to him. Then the most remarkable event occurred, John had noticed me and began to wave at me, smiling at me, I felt like my heart was going to explode, then it happened I collapsed onto the floor in shock grazing my knee.

As I got up from the floor, I ran down the cobbled path, trying to remove myself from the situation, it felt dangerous, it was a fantasy, what was I thinking? Why was I here? I asked myself.

At 2pm I arrived at the home of my son, a beautiful, stoned cottage with a yellow brick path leading to the bright red door, as I moved closer, the white Labrador jumped up, from the window and began to bark ferociously.

Suddenly, the red door sprung open, and an elderly lady dressed in a red dress, with her hair in curlers opened the door, the nanny of my son, she caught me off guard and I stepped back.

"Can I help you ma'am?

"No, I'm sorry I've got the wrong house." I panicked.

I watched as the mysterious lady looked at my leg in concern.

"Come inside your leg is bleeding, let me bandage that for you," she offered.

I looked down my leg and could see the pool of blood, I was reluctant to go in worried for my own sanity, but I was compelled to find out more, in my curiosity and confused state.

I walked into the dining room as the Nanny, Mrs. Harrington, went into the kitchen to grab the first aid kit. I looked at the photos in awe. There was a huge photo of John's parents on their wedding day, they looked like a beautiful Hollywood couple with their tanned faces, glistening hair and perfect physiques. The other photos including the couple with John making sandcastles on the beach, whilst another photo showed the family standing in front of Buckingham palace, and there were several baby photos of John, I realized in that moment I had to go, I needed help, I had finally lost it.

Mrs. Harrington rushed in, cleaning my wound and wrapping a bandage around my leg tightly.

"So, what brings a young girl like you to England, you're from Ireland right?"

"Yes," I smiled and began to cry as she wrapped the bandage neatly around my wound.

Then a car pulled up on the drive, stepping out of it was John with his adoptive mother. I ran out of the room, dropping the cup of tea on the floor leading to a great smash. I ran into the garden and at the end by the stone wall was a ladder. Mrs. Harrington proceeded to chase me, "Who are you? Come back here!" She yelled.

Just as she grabbed the end of the ladder, I managed to jump over the stoned wall landing on the grass in the park.

I could here Mrs. Harrington shouting for me to come back, I got up and ran as fast as I could, my heart raced, sweat poured down my face.

When I reached the hotel, I came to the realization that my son had a life I was not part of, it was a situation out of my hands, a world I could never be part of. I needed to see a counsellor, and get help, and I returned home, and received the help I needed joining a support group. I made friends with Debbie forty-year-old women who was sent to an asylum in Enniskillen. Debbie had managed to find romance and was married with four children and was now a paramedic. Debbie was the most resilient person I had ever met and used the pain of being in the asylum to help others through meditation, exercise, music, and framing negative thoughts into positive ones. I felt like I was on the road to recovery. I kept the meeting in London a secret from everyone, it was a moment of desperation a moment I wanted to forget.

Nursing grew difficult as time passed, more responsibilities were put onto me as time passed. I had to run wards on my own when the charge nurse called sick, I spent much of my spare time revising the anatomy and physiology of the human body, for my intense nursing exams and revision, my nursing mentors would constantly check my knowledge and ask me questions. I had spent my spare time working as a healthcare assistant, trying to get enough money to purchase a place of my own.

Everything was going well, I was trying to keep busy, then disaster struck on 1st July, I could hear Lucy crying hysterically on the sofa downstairs. I looked around looking for alcohol bottles, but could not find them, she had a picture in her hand.

"Lucy what's wrong?" I asked.

"I had a call this morning about Derek, he's dead!" She yelled.

"Dead?" I questioned, as my body collapsed in shock.

"Derek's mother Patricia rang this morning, he was Killed last night in a car accident crossing Bridgenorth Street, he died instantly.

My heart sunk, we had come through so much together, being in the asylum, the abandonment, and rebuilding our lives, losing Derek would destroy her.

I did not know what to say to her, there were no words to bring him back.

I took time off work and sat beside her, trying my best to comfort her,

Preparing her soup, preparing cups of tea, and checking she was ok, she was emotionally very weak, and I could not leave her alone.

I spent the next two days looking after Lucy, staying up at night to watch her, and making sure that she was comfortable.

Then on a hot Sunday Morning, as the crisp hot sun woke me up, I noticed that Lucy had gone, and her bike was gone. I was worried that she had disappeared in a manic state. I took my bike and raced up the cobbled road, calling out Lucy's name, but there was no sign.

I suddenly remembered going to the cliffside at St Michael's Park which led to the cliffside, overlooking a beautiful river. Two months previously we had a picnic under the oak tree overlooking the beautiful town, we were laughing and joking together, singing to escape the world.

As I ran up to the mountain top, I was left shaken as I saw Sara at the edge of the cliff standing with a half empty bottle of whiskey in her hand, swaying from side to side, narrowingly missing the edge.

"Step away from the edge, you have so much to live for!" I warned. I walked closer towards her, walking slowly, as I reached out my hand.

"I have lost my family, all of my friends, now the person I was going to marry, I have nothing!" Lucy raged, before throwing the bottle of whiskey over the edge.

"You still have so much to live for, we've been through so much you can't leave me on my own!" I warned.

It was then that I watched as Sara took a few steps back, and fatally fell off the cliff, hitting a tree, she died instantly. I stood at the edge of the cliff in tears, knowing that life was about to change forever.

Chapter 11: Meeting the

survivors.

Ten years had passed, and I was now a nurse on a general medical ward, I had worked so hard for financial independence, and I bought a beautiful stone cottage in Aukland Avenue, in a peaceful and quiet village just outside of town. The cottage was everything I dreamed of, with a white picket fence, a swing outside, and from my spacious bedroom was a view of the forest with the tallest oak tree, and on my balcony, I would sit reading books and writing my journal. My black Labrador Ben kept me company, we would race through the forest at night and watch the sunset, he would lay down next to me when I was upset, knowing when I was down, he was all I had.

I missed Lucy, I also felt a sense of guilt, I feel like I should have helped more, I felt immense guilt that she had ran to the cliff side and sunken so quickly into her depressive state.

I worked long twelve-hour shifts as a ward sister, I put everything into helping my patients, learning advanced CPR, reading advanced medical books to acquire more knowledge, and putting all my time into teaching my staff, and training them, to be the best nurses they could be. Nursing helped to keep my mind off the trauma of the asylum, and the abandonment by my parents. My mother had now passed, and I never received her forgiveness, but I was happy that I kept in regular contact with my siblings which helped to give me strength.

Then, one day as I walked up to the parish hall, I saw a sign, 'meeting for the Magdalene survivors.' The meeting was held on a Friday, and when I arrived at the meeting several women were present. Hayley, a headteacher, in her mid-forties, was sent to the asylum, after being accused of setting fire to the house of an elderly lady, in her town, but was set up an enemy at her school. Hayley had escaped the asylum four years after entering, concealing herself in a mail bag and gained a job as a waitress at a café in Enniskillen. After attending night school Hayley finished her education and eventually trained as a teacher, defying the odds in becoming a Headteacher. Hayley had tried for years to speak up for the rights of the girls in the asylum, but was ignored when she went to the press, for fear of causing trouble and lack of evidence. Hayley went on to Marry a high-profile banker, and had a son called Charles, her marriage later ended in divorce, which she blamed on her lack of trust and anger from being in the asylum.

I was amazed at Hayley's resilience, and her success showed in what she had achieved. I regularly visited Hayley's extravagant cottage and farm in which she owned two black horses. Hayley taught me to ride a horse and was my first real friend since Lucy. Whenever I was feeling low or upset, she invited me over and together we helped to heal each other.

Then there was Annie, a sixty-year-old woman, who had really struggled with her trauma following her exit from the asylum. Annie had been in the asylum for over thirty years, until her brother came to release her after years of waiting to be released. Annie went on a desperate search for her son Simon, and travelled to Poland to meet him after discovering that he was living with Lung cancer. After making the solo effort to travel, she was met with devastation when she arrived at his home. Simon had died from advanced cancer, and she never had the chance to say goodbye to him. Hayley and I could see the terror and devastation in her eyes, and we knew that the heartache had destroyed her life.

Gemma was 80 years old, when she arrived at the meeting, she was very angry, requesting everyone to be quiet and to pay attention every time she spoke. Gemma explained that her mother passed away at the age of sixteen and her father married a wicked woman, a woman who ordered her to clean constantly and ripped up her clothes.

In retaliation to the abuse she suffered, Gemma started to turn to petty crime, shoplifting at the sweet shop, setting fire to a friend's barn, and fell pregnant by the local drunk homeless man John. As soon as Gemma's pregnancy was revealed she was forced into the asylum. Then due to her poor behavior she spent most of her time in solitary confinement, often for swearing and hitting out at another girl's.

It was clear to see that Gemma still held onto anger, she carried on protesting weekly about the abuse she suffered, and would spend most of her time locked away in her house, shut away from everyone in the village.

It was very hard to talk positively or to try to talk about how we rebuilt our lives, when Gemma was so defiantly angry, but we were aware that some experiences were too tough to fully move on from.

Jean arrived at the support group dressed immaculately, in a red dress, with her hair tied in a bun, she seemed so prim and proper, so perfect but the reality was very different.

At the age of sixteen, Jean observed a local girl Terry forming an inappropriate relationship with the local priest, she spotted them holding hands ,and kissing in the priest's courtyard, early on a Saturday morning. Then in her curiosity she would spy on the priest's house which confirmed her suspicion that Terry was in a relationship with him. Jean could not hold her secret any longer and she went to the local convent, revealing her secret to the sisters.

The following day, the guards arrived at Jean's house, and she was forced out and moved to an asylum, in which she lost four years of her life. Jean commented that she was popular, achieved good grades, and always followed rules before entering the asylum. Jean had aspirations to study medicine, and worked hard to achieve her dream but being in the asylum took her dream away.

Once Jean was admitted into the asylum, she was treated to horrendous physical and mental abuse. Jean expressed that the nun's mentioned that she stood out with her good looks, and punished her by cutting her hair short, encouraging her to eat more, to make her plump, and depriving her of exercise to help her put on weight.

Jean struggled after her grandmother arrived to release her five years later. Jean lost her confidence and became a recluse, and worked as a cleaner in the local church, a job she took on for over forty years. Jean admitted that she was now living with manic depression, and spent the rest of her days feeling lonely and isolated.

Antonia at 88 years of age, was a very positive member of the group, who expressed her positivity despite the terrible experiences she endured.

At sixteen, Antonia started a relationship with Alberta, Alberta was her next-door neighbor from the Caribbean. When Antonia's Father found out about the relationship, he forced Antonia into her room each night, watching her every move.

Then Antonia decided to meet Alberta privately, and they made the fatal decision to runaway, and catch a boat to England, but her Father followed them to the port, and sending her to the asylum was the only way to keep Alberta and Antonia apart.

Antonia explained that she followed all the rules in the asylum, and when she left, she trained as an NHS secretary and married an Irish man called John, and they had two daughters. However, despite her new life, Antonia was still left abandoned by her family, and never received their forgiveness.

I had not spoken about my experiences in the asylum to anyone upon my release, it was too private, and they would not understand.

After meeting at the survivor's group, I would visit Lucy at her grave side and I would tell her about my life, what I had seen, and tell her about how much I missed her. I sent a letter to her family, after she passed, detailing her death, but they never replied, which made her pass more devastating.

Joining the survivors group made me look at the other journeys of people in the asylum and realized that I was now a strong person.

Achieving the status of ward sister was life changing, and a dream I felt I would never achieve. I was soon called the 'sister with the lamp' walking around the wards with my lamp on night shifts.

I remember how challenging my first night shift was, working with very challenging patients, whilst several of my staff had called in sick.

Jimmy, an eighty-year-old man, kept me entertained he would sing Motown songs during the day, he was a wedding singer, he had sung all over the world. Jimmy was admitted with shortness of breath, and we tried to encourage him to give up smoking, but I had caught him smoking in the bathroom, and admitted several warnings.

Then as I sat during the night at the desk he would dance with me to the song, 'my girl.'

What I liked about being a ward sister was hearing the stories of other patients, hearing about their trauma and helping them through. 90-year-old John was a young soldier in the war, and I was fascinated with his war stories. John spoke of being a scared seventeen soldier in the war. John spoke of being shouted at by the general in the trench and told to grow up, but he was lonely and missed his family, and was not prepared to live without his family.

John recalled the shocking first battle, he remembered running across no man's land, hiding behind a rock, he wrapped his coat around his head to hideaway. As The battle ended, he carefully carried his peers to the trenches, helping the medical team to wrap their wounds in bandages. John spoke of the terror of the soldiers, and they begged him to hold them, knowing that they were dying, and they did not want to die alone, John would hold the soldier's hand, he was with them to the end.

I lit a candle by John's bedside, helping him with his drink of water, and stroking his hand to sleep, on his bedside were war medals and a picture of him in his army uniform. John was receiving palliative care and died the next morning, but I felt so privileged to be with him in his final moments.

I had to observe the patient Harry closely, he sat in his seat confused and worried. Harry had been living on his own for ten years, and was admitted after setting fire to his kitchen. We were waiting for him to be assessed by social services. It was so difficult to support Harry, as he was confused to time and place and kept asking me what every noise was on the ward. Harry caused great panic when he hallucinated that was a rat roaming around the ward.

Tina in the side room kept shouting 'waitress, waitress,' Her UTI symptoms were worsening, and she was convinced that she was in a hotel.

I enjoyed the nightshift, being there for those that were lonely and needed the most support, being there for the most vulnerable people. Placing a comforting hand on a patient was enough to comfort them, whilst being a listening ear was all that someone needed.

When I arrived home, I would drink a cup of tea and collapse into a deep slumber, but this was my new life, and working helped me stop focusing on negative memories.

Chapter 12: The Letter

Sixty years passed since I escaped the asylum, and I felt I lived my life trying to recover from my teenage year's.

 I moved out of the rented flat, saving enough money to live in a cottage on River Town Road, the cottage was hidden by branches and a steel gate. I needed the privacy, I needed the safety of a locked gate.

I bought two golden Labradors and enjoyed their company, watching them run through the garden, and walking out onto by balcony, listening to the birds sing and feeling the morning breeze brush past my skin.

I battled loneliness through my work, working long hours as a ward nurse on a medical ward, eventually becoming a ward sister. As a nurse, I experienced taking part in cardiac emergencies, holding the hands of the dying patients, being there in their final moments, and watching patients recover after surgery, or achieve milestones such as being able to walk following a stroke. My patients were my therapy and my reason for living, my purpose.

I fought tirelessly for over fifty years to get justice for all of the fallen women in the laundries, I spoke to journalists, attended protests, and joined campaigns with other survivors. I was horrified when the mass graves were discovered, but also felt encouraged when the Magdalene girl's film was released. The truth was coming out, justice was prevailing, but I harbored so much anger knowing that the asylums continued to run until 1996, when the final laundry closed.

Mena continued to live in Ireland and with her husband she ran a successful printing business. Mal and Dom lived in England, and both worked in banking. Helena was a talented wedding singer and sang at wedding functions all over the world. Jack became a consultant doctor in Belfast, and Tom's finance business grew making over one million in profit. Cath moved to England, and ran a hairdressing company, but we lost touch over thirty years ago. Edith moved to Enniskillen, and ran a farm with her husband Eddie and lived a reclusive life.

My oldest sister Minnie lived in Bundoran, opposite the beach, she had five children, and over thirty Grandchildren, and was the queen of the family buying everyone extravagant presents.

My twin brother James died of natural causes ten years ago, my heart was broken, I felt like a piece of me was gone, I still talk to him every day, and follow his guidance.

I often thought about my son, wondering where he would be as a middle-aged man, wondering if I was now a grandma and if he ever thought about looking for me. I always thought about the son that had been taken away and the life he led. I did not expect to ever hear from him, but to finally reconnect over sixty years later felt like a miracle.

The postman pushed a blue envelope through the letterbox, and I looked at the envelope addressed simply to Mum, a personal letter from my son who tracked me down, now called Alexander, a letter which would change everything.

Alexander letter- 2015

I have waited years to speak to you and tell you my story, so I thought it was best to send it in a letter. I was able to track you down from the internet, I observed your photo at the Nursing awards in London in 2014, I instantly recognized you, from the hospital photo I have of you holding me, the photo kept by my adoptive parents.

I want you to know that I understand why you had to give me up for adoption, and I understand how difficult life was for you in the laundry, and I hope you are ok now, and have found ways to move past the awful situation.

My first memory was living in the children's home, which was unbelievably only a mile away from the laundry you were sent to. I remember we had a playroom with secondhand toys, including, bears, Dolls, and train sets. We would spend most of the time in the playroom, interacting with the orphans and developing communication skills.

Billy was my best friend in the orphanage, we did everything together, that is why it was so difficult when he was chosen for adoption and sent to a family in America. It happened frequently we would observe well presented couples, arriving in fur mink petticoats, and grand hats, coming to collect children to take them to a better place.

I remember standing in the hall in my old ragged white vest top and trousers, my eyes filled with tears, hoping I would be chosen, I waited patiently.

The bed was lumpy, the food was cold and basic, and we were confined to a strict regime, of prayer and silence after our play activities.

I remember when my adoptive parents arrived, Martin and Sally. Sally had bright blue eyes, and wild blonde curly hair, and stood in her black coat whilst Martin wore a three-piece suit. They were both Doctor's in their early forties, and unable to have children.

I was so frightened going to London on the ferry, it was the fear of the unknown, I missed the orphan voices and the security of being in the orphanage.

We lived in a beautiful three-story house in Piccadilly. In the dining room was the grand room, with a magnificent white piano, and a crystal chandelier. Adjacent to the dining room, was the dance hall, where they held lavish parties and grand balls.

Then the golden staircase led to the ten bedrooms, including seven bedrooms, a games room, a cinema room and a library. My bedroom had a king size bed, filled with toys, teddy bears and books. The view from my room was of the ten-acre garden, hidden by tall oak tree and a magnificent tree house.

Martin and Sally gave me the most wonderful childhood, I was educated at private school, we sang songs together in the evening, around a piano, I was given opportunities to play all the time.

Then at ten years of age they revealed that you were my mother Eileen, and they kept a photo of you in the hospital with me in my bedroom draw, I thought about you often and longed to find out about you.

At the age of eighteen I gained admission to medical school; my adoptive parents were so proud of me. Then a month before I left to start college, my adoptive parents died in an automobile accident and were killed instantly.

I struggled with the loss of my parents and threw everything into my studies, spending five years at medical school, my friends got me through the difficult times.

At twenty-five, when I went to Belfast train station, I observed a beautiful woman in a cream mink coat and her blond hair wrapped in a bun, and I realized that she left her bag on a bench. I grabbed the bag and ran onto the train, and found the woman her name was Mary a trained pharmacist. We hit it off instantly, sharing the same interests in pop music, films and going for a run.

Eventually, Mary moved in with me, in my childhood home, and we married and had three children, Elena, Hannah and Ben who eventually worked in the medical industry as doctors.

I progressed in the medical field and became a lead neurosurgeon, giving talks and lectures around universities all over the world, and winning awards for my work.

I know it has been over sixty years, but I hope you know that this letter comes as a general interest in finding you, and please find enclosed my address and phone number. I would love to talk to you and possibly arrange a meet with you, I look forward to hearing from you,

Alexander

I collapsed onto the floor by the door, I was shaking in shock, I had thought about Alexander every day of my life. Even though I had not seen him in sixty years, I knew now was the time to see him, life is so precious, and he was so important to me. That night I called Alexander and we spoke for an hour, I was in awe with his posh British voice, and in awe at his achievement as a doctor and the wonderful life he led. I did not expect for Alexander to come the following week on a visit, the moment I had waited nearly my whole life for.

Chapter 13: The reunion

I had been feeling sick for a few months, feeling

dizzy, extremely tired and struggled to get out of

the house. So, on a hot, warm, August day, when

I was feeling stronger, I decided to take a trip to

my favorite beach in Bundoran, I drove in my

jeep, taking sandwiches, cream scones, and a bottle of lemonade and my favorite deck chair.

I arrived at the beach at 10am, I reclined back in the chair, the sun warmed my skin, I could hear the waves crashing against the sea, the smell of the fresh sand, and savoring my flake ice cream, and it helped me drift into a state of contentment.

"Eileen Miller."

I turned around and there was Alexander, standing, dressed smartly in a white shirt, shorts, and curly blonde hair, he looked so much like my brother James.

I ran to him, and we embraced, I burst out into tears, with over sixty years of pent-up emotion.

"It is so wonderful to meet you finally, how did you find me?"

"I could see that you were not at home, so I thought I would try to find you at your favorite beach.

"You are so much taller than I thought you would be, I have dreamed of this day. Did you have a happy life despite the tragedies you faced?"

"My adoptive parents gave me everything, I was fortunate, they were both born into wealth. I followed a doctrine in which I had to read and study from the age of ten to eighteen. This strict doctrine helped me become a doctor, and achieve my dreams,"

"It is amazing to think we were both working in the NHS, I was working on a variety of medical wards, before running the cardiac ward as a ward manager for thirty years. It was tough, but it kept me going during the difficult times in my life. I always wanted to know Alexander how life was for you in the orphanage? I felt so guilty when you were taken away from me."

"It was a very strict environment, we had to play with toys that were broken, and we slept on uncomfortable beds and had cold dinners. It was difficult building a bond with the children, and watching them go to their new adoptive parents, much of my time was spent waiting, waiting to be chosen."

"I'm so sorry, but also so happy that your adoptive parents gave you the life I could not give you." I smiled.

We spent the afternoon walking together on the beach, feeling the breeze against our skin, and enjoying a scone as the bright sun shone on us. We reached the county Bundoran fair, and it was then that Alexander invited me onto the giant Ferris wheel. We laughed and sang as we sped slowly around in a circle. As we exited the ride, I began to feel dizzy holding onto the banister. I had to regain my composure, I could not let him

see how ill I truly was, and had to pretend I was

suffering from the effects of the ride.

When we arrived home, I enjoyed make

Alexander a roast dinner, and we spoke about the

future, and Alexander asked me if I would

consider moving to London, but it was a big step,

and I had big decisions to make.

After dinner I spoke with Alexander about my

harrowing time in the laundry, and he asked me if

I could show him my childhood home, the next

day, to find out more about my history. Alexander

was upset to hear of the slavery I endured, the

twelve-hour unpaid shifts, the punishments we

endured, and the stigma that we faced ever since.

The following day, we awoke, and we sat at the

breakfast table eating pancakes with delicious

golden syrup and green tea. I felt like I was

dreaming, having Alexander with me, I had finally felt happy again.

We Drove in Alexander's Mercedes down the country roads, singing along to pop songs, and taking in the air. We arrived back at my childhood home, and I could see that it had been rebuilt into a thatched cottage, housing a couple with five children, and a horse was in the barn. So much had changed, the house looked so modern, I could still see myself running down the cobbled road with my siblings, carefree and filled with so many dreams.

We carried on with our journey that morning and I was shocked when Alexander pulled up outside the St Bernadette laundry. I was shocked to see that it was still intact, but it looked burnt out, the windows were smashed, and the green vines towered over the front the building. The steel gates had been knocked down and were now on the ground. I sat in silence as all the memories came flooding back.

"I want to go in Alexander, give me ten minutes."

"Are you sure?"

"Yes,"

We made our way into the laundry and inside we observed the catastrophe, the walls were black and burnt out, all the tables in the dining room were crushed and broken, and the laundry work room was completely empty, with all the windows smashed.

I knew once I was in the laundry that I had to make my way up the now rusty spiral staircase, and observe the dormitory rooms. I arrived on the third floor and entered the fourth room, my old dormitory, the beds were still in the same position, and I could see on the wall, Anita's name carved into the wall, and under the bed was Bernadette's hairbrush covered in cobwebs. I could still hear the bell which was rung by the nuns in the morning, and I could imagine the girl's sleeping in their beds.

"This was you're room?" Alexander asked.

"This was my sanctuary, my escape from the abuse from the nun's, I would spend every night, laying in the bed, thinking of my family and thinking of you, but we learned to sleep, the work was so physically exhausting that we would collapse into a deep sleep most nights.

Suddenly the thought passed through my head, I had to see if the box I had buried under the floorboards was still in place.

I went under the bed where I slept previously, lifted up the floorboard to find my box filled with a picture of my family at the beach, a picture of Elvis with hearts drawn by Lucy, and diary entries I had kept in my notebook for over a year.

"I can't believe the box is here, after all these years, this was my secret box, the only power I had over the nun's and it made me feel in control, if they had found it would have been torn into pieces," I stammered.

"I can't believe the box is here after all these years, I'm so glad you got it back," Alexander smiled, looking on in amazement.

I knew it was time to go after being in the dormitory, I did not want to view the nurse office or the basement, some horrors were best left in the past, and I did not want top revisit again.

When we arrived back home, I felt like we had really got to know each other, and we were building the bond I had longed for.

That night, Alexander researched St Mary's asylum on the internet, and we discovered that it finally closed its doors in 1990.

We discovered that Sister Elizabeth was still alive, well into her nighties and resided in a care home, it felt cruel that she had lived for so long, whilst many of the women sent to the asylum had died in the laundry, or after, from the psychological stress. Alexander also discovered that that Bernadette had passed away ten years after I escaped, from malnutrition, I had often wondered what had happened to her, but knew due to her frailty that she would not live long.

The time had come the following day to say goodbye to Alexander, I watched as he stood by the taxi.

"Give yourself time to think about your decision to move, I have had the most wonderful few days being with you, I feel we have both found our missing puzzle piece," He smiled.

"Thank you for this time with you has been amazing, I want to thank you for showing me so much kindness and compassion, I finally have a son!" I smiled and we embraced each other.

I watched as Alexander drove off into the distance, I finally felt fulfilled and happy.

Suddenly I felt a sharp pain in my chest, and I could feel my head fill with pain. I shouted out for help and collapsed into the ditch, I could hear sirens coming towards me, before I went into a deep unconscious state.

I awoke in a cold, clinical, white hospital room, attached to a drip, and I observed the nurses rushing around through the glass window. Ten minutes later, a doctor and nurse arrived at the bed, and I managed to reposition myself to sit up, and began to return to normal.

It was then that Doctor John and Nurse Kelly sat beside me, Nurse Kelly held my hand, whilst Doctor John stood looking stern and emotionless with his clipboard. I knew it was bad news. Doctor John then explained that I had pancreatic cancer, and that it had spread to other parts of my body. Then the words terminal and no cure spun around my head, I was given treatment options to make me feel comfortable, I realized I should have sought help when I first fell ill, I tried to ignore how I felt, and thought that the illness would go away, but I did not expect such a poor diagnosis, I was thankful that the Doctor allowed me to return home the next day with medication.

I rang Alexander concealing the illness but confirmed that I wanted to move to London, and he accepted me with open arms, whilst knowing this was my final chapter, I knew I was moving to

a peaceful ending.

Chapter 14: Moving to London

I packed up all of my essential's photographs with my parents and siblings, my books, and my most sentimental clothes. As the taxi drove along the country roads, I realized I was saying goodbye to my past, taking one last look at my childhood home and the abandoned asylum.

I was so tired on the plane Journey; the strong tea and cheese sandwich could not keep my attention.

I arrived at the airport and observed Alexander, his wife Mary and my Grandchildren Elena, Hannah, and Ben standing with a sign which read 'welcome Eileen.' I was overcome with emotion and collapsed in tears, and we drove off in the Mercedes to his beautiful Mansion in London.

I was fascinating seeing my grandchildren, and seeing their interest in me left me fascinated, they were a part of me, and all so successful.

The town house was beautiful, with a ten feet waterfall towering over the entrance, with several orange trees scattered all around the front of the house. I was left speechless as I entered the house, the sparkling chandelier in the hallway lit up the house. The dining room with the tall grand piano, the flickering candles, and pictures of the family on holiday in Australia, Egypt, and America.

"Wow this is like a Hollywood film, this house is spectacular, it like a fairytale," I beamed.

"It has always been our perfect home!" Alexander cheered.

I travelled up the grand stairs, and marveled at the twenty rooms upstairs, including a magnificent library with thousands of books, including books by my favorite authors Charles Dickens and Stephen King. Adjacent to the library, was the cinema room with reclining red seats, a popcorn machine and a sweet machine.

Then Alexander introduced me to my room which had a four-poster bed, a gigantic circular couch, and a grand desk with several notepads, a draw filled with an assortment of pens and paints. It was the perfect set up for a writer.

I then stood by the window; it was heartwarming to watch the Labrador Penny running through the garden with her puppies travelling behind. Further into the distance I could see the glistening pool, covered by a glass building, and the tennis court. It truly was a fairytale dream, and I was waiting to wake up.

At 6pm we sat down to a beautiful roast dinner with the finest wine on the grand table.

"Well, I must say a beautiful Irish roast dinner in London, this is a turn up for the books!" I smiled, as the family laughed in unison.

"We waited for you to join our family for so long, we are so glad that we found you, and we have a surprise for you," Mary beamed.

I watched as Hannah disappeared outside of the room and returned with a six-week-old baby, her son Harry, and my Great grandchild, I was in awe and shock.

I held onto Harry in his blue blanket, and he stared up at me with his blue startling eyes.

"I can't believe this, I've been living on my own for so many years and now I have my son, Grandchildren and great Grandson in the same room, life cannot get any better.

After Dinner, I sat with my family in the living room watching old family videos, of baptisms, holidays, and my Grandchildren's wedding, it was great rebuilding a connection and feeling part of the family.

Then at 11pm I sat at the desk and put on the golden lamp, opened the notebook and began to write. I began to write my own story, from my life as a child, to my life in the asylum, to my life as a ward sister.

I could not stop writing as ideas and past stories came to me, I began to write frantically until 2am. I collapsed onto the bed and the velvet sheets felt so soft against my skin. It was so silent in the room, the only sound I could hear was the Grandfather Clock, chiming each hour. I had not felt so well in a long time. I knew that I would have to tell my family about my condition, it was not right to keep it a secret, but I wanted one day of normality, one day of cancer free talk before I would have to face the reality.

I awoke the next day, to a luxury breakfast, filled with choice including oatmeal bread, pancakes and a fresh jug of orange juice.

Then Alexander gave me a scrapbook filled with newspaper clippings from St Mary asylum, and pictures he was given from my adoptive family, and photos I passed on to him which he created into a collage.

"I'm so glad you followed journey, I just wish I would have been able to follow you," I beamed.

"Well, we have a big day for you today in London, we are going on our first family trip.

I wrapped up in my blue woolly coat and green hat, and I made my way with Alexander, Mary, and the children to the train station.

When we arrived at central London, we took a visit on the sightseeing bus, I was amazed observing the tower of London, Big Ben, parliament and Buckingham palace.

We spent time at Buckingham palace, taking photos, before going to Hyde Park for a picnic with cheese sandwiches, strawberries and a sponge cake and refreshing cold water.

"Did you ever meet anyone Eileen? Did you ever get married?

"Being in the asylum and after leaving, I lost my trust in people and struggled even to make friends, being in a romantic relationship did not appeal to me and I was never looking for one," I smiled. It was then that we were surrounded by the most beautiful white butterflies, I felt like it was a sign I had finally found my peace.

We walked through the streets of London, laughing and talking about famous landmarks, it was just what I needed a day of normality, and getting to know my family.

At 5pm we arrived at Frankie and Bennie's in waterloo. I got lost in my thoughts as I sat in the beautiful red seat. I was worried about telling Alexander about my cancer diagnosis, I did not want to spoil the family unit we had now created.

I ordered Lasagna with coke and a tower of fudge cake, drizzled in cream sauce, with strawberries pieces scattered on top. I took enjoyment in seeing a family opposite celebrate their mother's birthday, with confetti, music, and telling stories about the past.

In typical fashion it started to rain heavily, as we left the restaurant, and I was glad to return home, I was exhausted. Then as I sat at my desk at 10pm Alexander came into the room.

"There is something I need to tell you, something I should have told you from the start. I have pancreatic cancer."

"What have the doctors said? There must be a treatment, something they can do to support you?"

"There is nothing they can do; my condition is terminal. I have registered with the local hospital who will give me the pain relief I need."

I watched as Alexander sat on the bed, a tear rolled down his cheek, I could see the shock and sadness in his face.

"I need you to be happy, I love being here, it was the best decision I made, but I can't do this without you, being here is paradise, writing my memoir, overlooking the beautiful view of the garden, and eating dinner with the family is what I always wished for." I smiled.

"If you need anything just ask, no request is too big I want you to be completely comfortable.

Chapter 15: Writing memories

It was easier now to carry on, being open about

my illness. Alexander would leave early most days

for his clinics, and I was alone in the house until

later afternoon. In the morning the nurses would

come in and administrate my pain relief, and ensure that I felt comfortable.

For the rest of the day, I felt like a child again, I was free to do what I want.

I would spent an hour in the library reading an assortment of books, then I would spent an hour or so in the cinema room watching my all-time favorite films, including 'it's a wonderful life,' and the 'wizard of oz,' although often I would find that I collapsed into a deep sleep, struggling to maintain my attention. Then before the family returned, I would sit in the garden catching the sun's rays with a refreshing glass of water.

My bedroom was my sanctuary, and whilst writing my memoir at night, all the memories came back to me from the past.

My most wonderful memory from the laundry involved a girl called Susan Becker, a girl who had escaped the asylum five years previously. Susan had planned to break into the asylum with her friends to wage war, pressing the fire alarm button, and releasing all of the girl's, the ultimate act of rebellion.

I remember observing her at 6pm, as the sun was going down, I observed her with her friends holding a ladder and bringing it towards the wall. I watched in awe as the girls climbed over the wall, quickly, I could see the look of determination on Susan's face, full of venom and hungry for revenge.

I waited anxiously for the girls to enter the asylum, and I knew that chaos was about to ensure.

Moments later, the fire alarm rang out, we realized we had to leave the dormitory with immediate effect. Suddenly, there was a stampede of girls running from the dormitory, Susan's friends had stacked several tables outside the door in an tempt to prevent the nun's and guard's escape.

We cheered and ran through the corridor, and when we reached the entrance, we observed that the front gate was open. So many of the girls in the dormitory ran for the freedom, and as Susan and her friends closed the steel gates. They stood with their water bombs, and we watched as they threw the water bombs at Sister Elizabeth and the guards, I could see the anger and look of terror in Sister Elizabeth's face.

"I know who you are Susan, and you will not get away with this!" She yelled.

"Run girl's, run!" Susan cheered.

As I hurried with Lucy, I watched as Susan ran forward to her automobile, and drove off into the distance. We ran with the other girls through the cornfield, as the red velvet sky lit up in front of us. The guards were too fast driving in three cars, they managed to catch up with us, and cornered the girl's, we were all unable to escape. What started as a night of triumph, and glory, our dreams were burst as we returned to the laundry. Susan was an inspiration to us all, she inspired my fight for freedom and fight to succeed.

In a break from writing, I observed the scrapbook created by Alexander, including photos from his graduation, his awards evening and photos on holiday with his children, it reminded me of the life I missed out on, but it helped to put the pieces together.

I was not aware that the following week would turn into a disaster, I was admitted into hospital with suspected sepsis, I remember going into a deep sleep, and dreamt of being back with my siblings and parents, sitting around the breakfast table eating porridge, it was the most happiest memory, singing Irish folk songs with my sisters, racing with my brothers on the cobbled road, and never being alone, there was always someone to talk to.

A week later I awoke from the coma, and the doctors explained to me that I was lucky to survive but that my condition had progressed. I knew I did not have long left, and I was so happy that Alexander fought for me to stay at his home, instead of spending the remainder of my time in a hospice.

I needed to finish my memoir, spend more time with my family and speak to my siblings, I was not ready to go yet there was still more to do.

Chapter 16:The Lost Magdalene child

I was so happy to have private time with

Alexander at the hospital, a day before I was

discharged. Alexander entered the side room, with

a gift, wrapped in red wrapping paper. I

apprehensively opened the present, and found

that Alexander had written his own book, in a scrapbook style, entitled the 'lost Magdalene child.'

"I was so thankful we have read your story, so I decided to make my own book about my life, with pictures and stories from my childhood."

I was amazed that Alexander had spent the time creating a book for me, we sat together with our cup of tea, chocolate cake, and dimmed the lights, it was the perfect night.

Alexander detailed the dark memories he had of the asylum, the cold damp and wet conditions. All of the children wore white ragged clothes, and were scorned when there was dirt on the clothes. Each night the children would line up for cold baths and showers, and they shivered under a single blanket.

In the playroom Alexander detailed that he enjoyed playing with firetrucks and toy soldiers. In the library room Alexander would look out of the window, which overlooked St Mary's asylum, and he would look out at the asylum and observed the Magdalene girl's who the staff described as 'bad girls.' My blood went cold, knowing that alexander was so close, after thinking he was so far away.

I looked at the picture of Alexander in his ripped white outfit, his face was pale and worn, and he looked malnourished. The toys in the gym room looked broken and old, the other children looked similar thin and malnourished.

I observed that Alexander had a strict but happy childhood. After school he had a strict curriculum to follow, consisting of Math's, English and Science, he explained that he missed out on social activities due to the strict study regime. In between studying, Alexander enjoyed playing tennis with his father, and swimming to help relieve his stress.

I cried reading the struggle Alexander had following his parent's death. After they passed, he descended into drinking alcoholism, drinking at school, and drinking at home to numb the pain.

The breaking point came when he was found by the cleaner passed out in the pool, after overdosing on tablets. It was then that Alexander realized he had to carry on, and he battled against the loneliness.

I marveled at the stories he had described his time as a doctor in London. It was amazing to see that he took the lead when supporting teenagers involved in a car crash. Suddenly, he had to take the lead, compressing the bleeding, taking vital observations and whilst one of the teenage boy's was taken to emergency surgery the other teenager went into cardiac arrest. It was then that Alexander had to take the lead, starting compressions and leading staff into taking compressions, Alexander was thankful that both boys survived, against the odds.

I enjoyed reading about Alexander, Mary, and my grandchildren's holiday adventures. The family appeared to be thrill seekers visiting famous theme parks in America and France, and taking part in extreme watersports, and safaris.

In Australia disaster struck when the family went canoeing, the weather took a turn for the worse, and Alexander was catapulted from the boat into the rough sea. As his family looked desperately for him, he banged his head on a rock, and he was carried along in the rough sea. Two days later Alexander was discovered at an abandoned shore and airlifted to hospital, he survived against the odds.

I spent hours talking to Alexander and it was great to have time alone time with him after so long, I had missed out on such a big chunk of his life, I was now able to see into his world, I had

missed out on so much and lived a life of

loneliness, and despite being terminally ill, I had

never been so happy.

Chapter 17: Saying Goodbye

I felt like time was ticking and I had little time to complete all the activities I wanted.

When we arrived home, we returned to spectacular snow three feet deep, and I advised

Alexander that I wanted to go outside. The ten-acre garden was filled with snow, it was magnificent. When I was a child, I remembered my siblings running outside, we would make the biggest snowman possible. We would use all of the items we could find, buttons, fruits, a scarf, chocolates and beads and paint to create the most beautiful snowman. We had so little, this was a huge treat for us, a time when we escaped the dull and dreary rain which plagued us almost all year around.

"It is too cold mother, you will catch your death," Alexander warned.

"I am all wrapped up, I will be fine, I want us to make a snowman, the biggest one!"

We started to build the snowman and then the Grandchildren joined, building a gigantic snowman, it brought us together and helped to take my mind off the terminal news, I almost felt like a child again and carefree.

I was treated like a queen the next day, Andrew organized for a cook, Emma, to serve me my delicious pancakes with golden syrup, orange juice and crumpets.

Then the nurses would come to give me my medication, and I was so happy to be feeling so strong.

I cherished each moment, opening the window and hearing the birds chirping, drinking a fresh glass of water, and the sunlight shining on my skin, everything felt so important, and worries appeared pointless.

After medication, I would sit at my desk writing my memoir. When I closed my eyes, I was back in the asylum, I was sixteen and a helpless child. I could see Elizabeth's wicked green eyes and greasy hair wrapped up in a bun, ready to inflict terror. I could feel my hands running through

Bernadette's curly brown hair. I could still see myself running with Lucy through the beautiful cornfield, the air brushing past us, my heart was racing, filled with adrenaline, I had so much fight in me, determined to escape.

Christmas arrived and it was like a fairytale Christmas, one I had always dreamed off. The Christmas tree was over ten feet high, with sparkling multicolored lights, tinsel was wrapped up the golden staircase, and an assortment of ornaments al over the house. Under the tree were hundreds of presents wrapped under the tree, in red wrapping paper, tied up with a black string.

The dinner was perfect, a full turkey dinner and mash, and an assortment of crackers. I felt weak, and sick following my medication and could not consume the whole meal, so I took breaks in between eating.

I was so thankful in having my family around me for the first time, and I wanted to raise a toast.

"I want to thank you all for giving me the best Christmas I could ask for. I waited over sixty years to meet Alexander, now I am a great Grandma. On the middle of the table is my memoir, my story, that Alexander helped me write, from my time as a sixteen-year-old girl abandoned in the laundry, to my fight for freedom and achieving my dream of becoming a nurse. I want my story to live on, and I hope you all think of me positively," I smiled.

That night we sat around the burning log fire, the snow was gently falling outside, we were wrapped up with blankets wrapped around us, taking it in turns burning our marshmallows in the fire. We sang, 'I'm dreaming of a white Christmas,' and a tear fell down my cheek, I was so happy so content, for the first time in my life I had everything I wanted.

Chapter 18: The final goodbye

Two months after Christmas, I appeared to deteriorate and I now required nasal specs oxygen to help me breathe, and Alexander had a nurse that supported with my care needs, including medication and personal care. My bed was moved to the window, so I had a view of the ten-acre garden and magnificent water fountain.

My radio which played classical music and my album my Enya helped to keep my spirits up. On February 1st I was given the biggest surprise by Alexander, he stood outside my room and requested that I close my eyes and when he asked me to open, I observed my brothers and

Sisters standing around the bed. Mena arrived with flowers, Mal and Dom had a cassette player in their hands and a cd player, cassettes of all the songs we listened to as a child. I was amazed that Tom had travelled all the way from Australia to see me, Edith and Jack came with a basket of cakes, and Helena came towards me and embraced me tightly. Lewis and James had passed away although we could still feel their presence.

I cried, it was the first time we had all been together since I was sixteen, and it felt like we had transported back into a time machine. Dom and Mal were telling jokes and still acting childish, Edith was the homemaker, making sure everyone was eating and drinking. Tom described his amazing tales in Australia, Helena was constantly singing folk Irish songs, and Jack was reminiscing about the past. My sister Minnie was unable to come due to her back problems, but we had planned to talk through the face time. Suddenly, I was talking to my siblings about my time in the asylum, and they listened in horror and guilt, but also described how they missed me every day, and how friends and family members stopped visiting due to the stigma I caused for my family.

I had never been so happy to have my family with me Alexander had ordered a curry for everyone with the trimmings and ice cream for everyone. At night everyone slept in their sleeping bags, and I felt so comforted. In the middle of the night Mena crept towards me and held my hand.

"You're going to be ok, don't be afraid to die Eileen, you have had such a wonderful life, you have saved lives, you're a survivor."

"I have my son, my family that I never dreamed I would have, in a way I feel like my life is just beginning."

"We will all be with you one day in heaven, you have been a fighter all your life and we are so thankful for you." Mena smiled.

That night I went to sleep hearing the gentle noises from my siblings, and the wind brush past the window. I still did not want to give up I was desperate to survive.

The next morning, I heard the door creak, and looked on in awe as my oldest sister Minnie opened the door, and struggled through with her walking stick, making her way slowly.

"I can't believe you made it!" I gasped.

"Well, I could not miss the opportunity to see my little sister, and meet my wonderful nephew! Look at you Eileen, living in this wonderful mansion, you finally got your fairytale, and no one deserves it more than you!" She gasped.

Then Minnie took out a gift a photo taken outside my home two weeks before I was sent to the laundry. I was dressed in a white dress and James was carrying me on his shoulders, the sun was shining, and we were all laughing, it was my final moment of happiness before life changed for everyone.

As we all sat around the breakfast table enjoying our pancakes and golden syrup, Helena started singing, 'everything I do I do it for you,' my favorite song and we all joined in unison, singing brought us all together connected us as a family, having my siblings around made coping with the illness easier.

When my family left, I was left with Alexander in the dining room, we watched my favorite film 'It's a wonderful life,' I reflected on my life, and knowing that despite all the battles and struggles I finally found my peace.

"This is my favorite film," Alexander beamed

"Mine too, and despite all of my struggles I really have had a wonderful life!"

Chapter 19: The Magdalene asylums

As part of my dissertation in 2012 I visited Ireland to interview a Magdalene survivor called Maria, and learnt all about the devastation and abuse inflicted on women in the asylums. I joined a survivor's group in Enniskillen, hearing the stories from a range of women, who all described the physical and mental abuse they endured.

The Magdalene asylums ran from the 19th and 20th century and housed fallen women and were named after Mary Magdalene. Women were mainly sent to the Magdalene asylum for having children out of wedlock, and women who were deemed to be promiscuous, whilst other women entered the asylum to keep away from prostitution, as single mothers, as there were no welfare benefits, so women had no choice but to enter the institutions. The Magdalene asylums were seen to divert women from vicious lives and expanded due to supporting free labor. Asylums grew due to a rise in poverty, unemployment rates were rising, and overcrowding was a problem, the government was focused on moral reform and not social reform. Women were sent to the asylum for the purging of their sins. Over 30,000 women were sent to the asylums between the 19th and 20th century. There was a 'veil of secrecy' despite repeated requests for information, records of women were hidden, 'women did not matter, or did not matter enough.'

Working in the laundry each day was seen as a way for the women to clear their sins. Women were forced to work unpaid and in often very difficult conditions, with little breaks, and lack of substantial food, which inhibited their ability to complete tasks fully. Women were enforced to wash the laundry of the public, prisons, schools and from the religious orders.

Women complained about the poor treatment bestowed upon them by the nuns and the religious elders. Women would have their hair cut, and their names changed and would often be punished on a regular basis. Women complained of being hit, whipped, locked in rooms, and suffered both physical and mental abuse.

The final laundry closed in 1996, and after the closure the truth about the asylums were revealed. A septic tank was found containing the human remains of babies which were buried in the grounds of the asylum. The discovery of the mass grave in a Dublin Covent in 1993 led to an increase in media attention.

In 2013 a state apology was issues which agreed that the Magdalene asylums were places of abuse, and a £50 million compensation fund was set up for survivors.

The legacy of the Magdalene asylums lives on in the children that were adopted, and those that survive and still fight for justice.

There have been several media interpretations based on the Magdalene asylums including the Magdalene sisters, a film about the lives of four incarcerated women. A documentary sex in a cold climate in 1998, detailed the abuse suffered by women including sexual abuse, and focused on the reasons why people were sent to the asylum from promiscuous behavior to looking 'too pretty.'

The end

Printed in Great Britain
by Amazon

26541145R00155